LIFE AFTER DEATH

Considers whether mankind possesses the capacity to
live on after death and looks at the evidence for
post-mortem communication.

By the same author
MIND OVER MATTER

LIFE AFTER DEATH

The CASE FOR SURVIVAL OF BODILY DEATH

by

D. Scott Rogo

Series Editor: Hilary Evans

GUILD PUBLISHING
LONDON

This edition published 1986 by
Book Club Associates
by arrangement with
Thorsons Publishing Group Limited

Printed and bound in Great Britain

Contents

Introduction

The idea that we will survive the shock of death is an ancient and perennial one. Each and every world culture and religion teaches the doctrine. The prevalence of this view is so widespread that Sir James G. Frazer, who pioneered the modern study of anthropology in the nineteenth century, felt compelled to find an explanation for it in his classic *The Golden Bough*. His theory was that when early man dreamed of the dead, he misinterpreted the phenomenon as experiences with direct contact. In the long run, though, Frazer's proto-psychological theory could not explain all aspects of the immortality belief. It could not explain why different peoples developed such varying concepts of the afterlife. Some primitive societies gradually adopted the notion of a heavenly realm similar to our earthly life. Reincarnation and the transmigration of the soul took hold in Africa and the Orient; while the early Christians were hopelessly divided between spiritual versus physical resurrection.

Probably the most meaningful rebuttal to Frazer's theory came by way of Andrew Lang's *The Making of Religion*, which was also published around the turn of the century. Lang was an Irish folklorist fascinated by the tales of ghosts, apparitions, and poltergeists that abound in the lore of different societies. He eventually came to believe that these stories represented genuine psychic experiences, which led him to postulate that early man came to believe in immortality because of *real*, not *imagined*, contact with the superphysical world.

This present book will examine whether there exists any basis for the approach outlined by Lang. There can be no doubt but that mankind has long nurtured a sacred belief in life after death; nonetheless, there exists a great chasm between belief and proof. This is where, as Lang so rightly saw, the study of psychic phenomena comes into play. Such phenomena as apparition and ghosts, the messages received through trance mediums, the visions of the dying, the testimony of so-called 'astral' projectors, and other similar manifestations bear crucially on the issue of survival. If the human experience of day-to-day living includes direct contact with the world of the dead, there seems little reason to explore hypothetical psychological roots for the belief.

Despite this obvious point, conventional science has long shied away from studying the phenomenon of death and what lies beyond it. Only within the last two decades has the scientific study of the death experience, *thanatology*, emerged as a separate field of study from the main body of conventional psychology. Science and psychology hitherto merely viewed the death experience as a deep dark foe and not as a valid area of inquiry. The *only* scientific discipline that has ever concerned itself with the study of human immortality has been psychical research, or parapsychology, and probably a majority of scientists would object to this being called scientific. This interest dates back to the nineteenth century, and the story of how the field first became involved in the study of survival will be told in Chapter 1. Since parapsychology has only attained a precarious foothold within the scientific community during the last twenty-five years, suffice it to say that its discoveries about life after death have never made much of an impact on science or culture in general. But this in no way denigrates the importance of the data uncovered by the first scientific parapsychologists. They began their work by studying apparitional experiences, hauntings, and the visions of the dying, and then turned to the study of trance mediums, who purported to bring through discarnate intelligences directly. These endeavours were challenging and frustrating, since the first researchers were not clear about what criteria could be used to prove life after death.

Today, a hundred years have passed since the first psychical researchers attempted to explore the issue of life after death. The search for this evidence has now spread to psychology, physics, and even biology. New lines of evidence are coming to the forefront of research, including studies of out-of-body experiences, the reports of people who have 'died' but who have 'come back', and the memories of young children who claim to recollect their previous incarnations. All these phenomena will be considered during the course of this book.

This short volume will be concerned primarily with the evidence for survival — both whether mankind possesses the capacity to live beyond death and whether post-mortem contact has ever been reliably achieved. This approach has been adopted to the exclusion of other issues which arise from the study of human survival. Among these, for example, is the whole question of conceptualizing what the 'next world' will, or might, be like. It is my own view that we really are in no position to speculate on this matter without becoming self-indulgent. The evidence about life after death is too contradictory and beset by too many problems

Throughout history mankind has cherished the idea that we survive death in some form. This seventeenth-century Italian engraving shows the ghost of a drowned sailor revisiting his astonished wife. (Mary Evans Picture Library)

to make such speculation meaningful.

For those readers primarily interested in the problem of anticipating the nature of the 'next world', it should be noted that two notable attempts have been made to draw-up cartographies of this world beyond. Both have been based on evidence gleaned from psychical research. The first came in 1961 when the late Dr Robert Crookall, then a retired British scientist, showed in his book *The Supreme Adventure* that the descriptions

Dr Robert Crookall amassed many hundreds of testimonies from people who claim experiences of life on other planes. (Mary Evans Picture Library)

of the afterlife offered by astral projectors, near-death survivors, and mediumistic 'communicators' were mutually consistent. This idea was reinforced in 1981 when Paul Beard, a British spiritualist leader, showed similar consistencies within the communications of a handful of credible mediums. (This data was presented in his highly readable book *Living On*.) Both researchers drew up a picture of a world beyond death graded into several realms according to one's spiritual level, and ending in a mysterious 'second death' of some sort.

The problem with this approach was that both researchers based their cartographies on the *ad hoc* and *post hoc* selection of data. They also drew primarily from spiritualistic sources, or sources at least inspired by popular spiritualism. This was a critical miscalculation, for by the turn of the present century spiritualist philosophy had already developed a structured theology about the nature of the world beyond. This view was greatly inspired by, and modelled on, the writings of Emmanuel Swedenborg, an eighteenth-century Swedish mystic. His cartography was based on his personal visionary experiences, and was actively incorporated into spiritualism by many of the first leaders of the movement in the United States. The reason why communications received through so many subsequent psychics are so similar could be that they were based upon common sources of information, bias, and inculturation.

Because the survival issue is so confusing and complicated, we shall in this book confine our attention to the basic problems of whether belief in immortality is logical, and whether any direct evidence can be marshalled in support of the notion. We shall start by making a brief survey of the history of survival research, and will go on to explore more recent approaches to the controversy. The final chapter will outline how I have personally come to view the issue, and describe cases which I feel point most directly to survival.

1.

Psychical Research and the Survival Controversy

The Case of James Kidd

One of the more curious chapters in the history of American jurisprudence dates back to 1967, when an eccentric Arizona prospector named James Kidd was declared legally dead. He had disappeared into the desert surrounding Phoenix in 1949. Such an occurrence probably would have gone unnoticed by the papers and the public . . . except for a bizarre catch to the case. When the prospector disappeared, he left about $175,000 in cash and stocks in his bank account. He also left behind a handwritten will dated 2 January 1946 which stated, in part, that the bulk of his estate should go towards '. . . research of some scientific proof of a soul of the human body which leaves at death . . .'

When news of the will was made public, it caused somewhat of a furore. Soon the superior court in Phoenix was deluged with claimants, each hoping to profit from the will. There were psychics, churches, philosophers, research institutes, and a variety of eccentrics, all laying claim to the money. The hearings held by the court over the next few months were filled with deep philosophical discussions as well as humour. One 'psychic' woman from Los Angeles demonstrated for the court how her 'spirit guide' could answer questions through her, while she kept a hair-drier running so she couldn't hear what was being asked! A philosophy teacher from a junior college in California testified that he could prove the existence of the soul through logic, while the Arizona-based Barrow Neurological Institute petitioned to conduct brain research with the funds. Parapsychologists were intrigued by the will as well, and both the American Society for Psychical Research (from New York) and the Psychical Research Foundation (from Durham, North Carolina) sent representatives to testify.

The hearings finally became known as 'The Great Soul Trial', and the court's final decision was rather anti-climactic. Judge Robert J. Myers awarded the funds to the Barrow people, arguing that the money would best be used in some practical research pursuit.[1]

The decision enraged several of the claimants, who pointed out that the Institute had previously disqualified itself by its own testimony. Representatives sent by the Institute explained during the hearings that they wouldn't conduct research on the soul, so the critics were justified in their protests. Eventually both the American Society for Psychical Research and the Psychical Research Foundation, which had been founded in 1960 expressly to research the survival problem, filed appeals. The state supreme court was more sympathetic than the superior court, and after reviewing the case, Judge Myers was ordered to re-rule his decision. This left him little alternative but to award the money to the A.S.P.R., since the Society aptly demonstrated during the earlier hearings that it was historically concerned with finding evidence for life after death. They, in turn, decided to share the bequest with the P.R.F.

The strange case of James Kidd and his will provided parapsychology with a curious precedent. It publicly and (in a sense) legally acknowledged that the question of life after death could be scientifically studied. It also established that the science of parapsychology was best qualified to undertake the challenge. The re-ruling of the lower court was probably influenced by the testimony of the late Dr Gardner Murphy, who was the president of the A.S.P.R. at the time and also an eminent psychologist. Murphy took pains to explain during his testimony that the field had long devoted itself to the study of apparitions, deathbed visions, mediumship, and other psychic phenomena. These were rare occurrences that suggested that occasionally we among the living can glimpse the world unseen. Now the court found itself agreeing on the matter.

But if parapsychology has been exploring the survival question for so long, why is the case for life after death still open? For, while a rich historical literature exists on the subject, the ultimate proof of life after death remains elusive.

The Foundations of Survival Research

In order to understand the complexities of the survival issue, you must first understand a little about the history of psychical research. Parapsychology today is an experimental science, and most professional researchers devote themselves to testing people in the laboratory for telepathy, clairvoyance, precognition, and mind over matter. This is actually only the newest face parapsychology has adopted during its short history, in its search for scientific respectability. The science of parapsychology actually dates back to the 1880s, which was an era before the advent of complicated statistics, psychophysiology, and the other tools used by parapsychologists today. Psychical research in those early years was a more philosophical and existential pursuit, since it emerged from a society very different from that of today.

Several factors contributed to the way culture was forced to change during the Victorian age, and these factors naturally influenced the way in which psychical research first developed. This was an age where science and scientific achievements were challenging the religious authority that had guided European thought for the previous five hundred years. The nineteenth century was an age of industry and invention, and many people believed that science, and not religion, would salvage mankind and prove him master of the universe. It didn't help matters either when Charles Darwin, the brilliant British scientist and thinker, came forth with *The Origin of Species by Means of Natural Selection* and (later) *The Descent of Man*. Darwinian thinking implied that man was merely a part of the existing world order and not set apart from it. Darwin's discoveries demonstrated that man did not suffer a spiritual 'fall' from Divine grace when he came to inhabit the earth, but merely evolved from lower life forms. This represented a challenge to Christian authority, which taught that man must fight to regain the spiritual status he lost at the beginning of time. During these years, scholars in Germany were also showing that even the Bible itself was not an infallible document, but could be critically analysed like any other piece of literature. And what they were uncovering was disturbing to the religious establishment.

What resulted was a society which, for the first time in years, would not adopt a spiritual world-view simply on the basis of religious dogma. Science was raising mankind above the gods, and it looked as though religion would have to adopt the methods of science in order to prove such doctrines as the soul and its immortality.

It was also during these critical years that a small sect came surging out of the United States. Spiritualism was a small religious movement whose roots dug deeply into the American culture of the 1840s and '50s. The development of the movement dated back to 1848, when several eyewitnesses were able to observe some poltergeistic antics in a cottage located in Hydesville, New York. The outbreak consisted chiefly of intelligent rappings, and focused on two teenaged girls living in the house. Margaret and Kate Fox, whose father was a local farmer, were soon travelling throughout the East demonstrating their power to 'bring through' the raps from the spirit world. These demonstrations piqued the interest of the scientific community as well as the general public, who saw in the paranormal the basis for a new religion . . . a religion which taught that communication with the dead was a common reality. Whether or not these first two 'mediums' were genuine or fake is really inconsequential, for spiritualism was now on the rise.

The Fox sisters cause a table to levitate at Rochester in the 1850s; such physical
feats were supposed to be caused by the spirits, thus giving evidence of survival.
(Mary Evans Picture Library)

What so appealed to the American public was that spiritualism appeared to be 'scientific' religion. It didn't base its theology on dogma or authority, but taught that each seeker could prove its main tenets for him or herself. The sceptic merely had to procure the services of a good psychic or trance medium.

The rise and spread of the spiritualist movement not only influenced popular culture, but came to the attention of the British intellectual establishment as well. The advancement of spiritualism in England occurred at about the same time that a number of British philosophers, loosely connected by their association with Cambridge University, were grappling with religious doubts of their own. Chief among these thinkers was Professor Henry Sidgwick, who was an influential philosopher and a professor at the university. His fellow intellectuals included his former pupil F. W. H. Myers, and Edmund Gurney, a Cambridge graduate and a musicologist of no mean merit.

These intellectuals were acutely distressed by the changes they were seeing in British culture and thinking. They were the sons of ministers and had been brought up to cherish Christian values and beliefs. It troubled them to see society turning from the old doctrines, but at the same time, they realized that these changes were logical in the radically changing world. They were aware that society was about to be deluged in a wave of atheism and materialism, which they felt would mark the decline of society. So they soon became committed to finding a way of re-establishing the Christian order. Since they could no longer rely on polemics or philosophical reasoning, they found themselves in quite a quandary. And it was at this time that they began casting a still-suspicious eye at the spiritualist movement which had emigrated to England in 1852. The Cambridge group finally decided that it was in this arena that they could make their most important gains. For if the supernatural could be scientifically demonstrated, they believed, their findings could be used to reject Victorian materialism.

It should be pointed out, though, that the Cambridge group was not out to 'prove' spiritualism. The members merely reasoned that if the phenomena of spiritualism were genuine, these strange events would reconfirm the spiritual nature of man. Some critics of the group's work also charged that these thinkers were emotionally committed to finding proof of life after death. This, however, was hardly the case. Professor Sidgwick and his colleagues were eager to find scientific evidence with which they could rebut the tide of materialism popular in their day. But they also realized that this evidence would have to be strong enough to influence any objective critic, as well as satisfy their own challenging doubts.

This, in fact, is one of the reasons why the survival controversy has never been resolved within parapsychology. The founders of the science soon learned that finding proof of life after death, an issue that indeed became central to them, was not as easy as solving a problem in logic or the solution to an algebraic equation.

The most important outcome from these years of search and questioning came in 1882, when the Cambridge group joined forces with several of the more critical members of the spiritualist movement. Together they founded the Society for Psychical Research, which became the first scientific body devoted to the study of the paranormal. The goal of the S.P.R. was to investigate reports of psychic phenomena, establish criteria for what constituted evidence, and then determine the nature of these events. The Society undertook these studies in a critical frame of mind, and many notable figures in British history joined forces with it. These included several eminent scientists as well as a few political leaders.

The science of modern parapsychology was born through the endeavours of the S.P.R. In time even the spiritualist elements fell away from the Society as the original Cambridge group began applying more and more critical standards to their studies. For better or for worse, the S.P.R. eventually freed itself from its early religious associations. It became essentially a society devoted to separating fact from fiction and fraud in the study of psychic phenomena.

The founders of the S.P.R. set about to study a rich variety of paranormal phenomena, not all of which directly related to the survival problem. They investigated cases of telepathy occurring in everyday life, spearheaded experimental research on thought-transference, looked into poltergeist cases, and were fascinated by the study of hypnosis. But the central concern of the S.P.R. was with the survival issue.

Apparitions and the Case for Survival
Since the first psychical investigators conducted a fair amount of field research, it wasn't odd that their first evidence for survival emerged from the day-to-day experiences of the British public. The S.P.R. founders were interested in collecting and studying cases of spontaneous ('real life') psychic experiences, and by 1886 they were amassing a great number of cases of telepathy, apparitional experiences, and other psychic anecdotes. What so impressed these great thinkers was the number of crisis apparition reports included in their data. These were cases in which an apparition was seen at the same time that the person who projected it actually died. Thirty-two such cases were included in their collection, and the S.P.R. leaders felt that an in-depth investigation of these reports

might help resolve the survival issue.[2]

The following report is typical of these early cases. The report was dated 20 May 1884:

> I sat one evening reading, when on looking up from my book, I distinctly saw a school-friend of mine, to whom I was very much attached, standing near the door. I was about to exclaim at the strangeness of her visit when, to my horror, there were no signs of anyone in the room but my mother. I related what I had seen to her, knowing she could not have seen, as she was sitting with her back towards the door, nor did she hear anything unusual, and was greatly amused at my scare, suggesting I had read too much or been dreaming.
>
> A day or so after this strange event, I had news to say my friend was no more. The strange part was that I did not even know she was ill, much less in danger, so could not have felt anxious at the time on her account, but may have been thinking of her; that I cannot testify. Her illness was short, and death very unexpected. Her mother told me she spoke of me not long before she died . . . She died the same evening and about the same time that I saw her vision, which was the end of October, 1874.

It soon fell to Edmund Gurney to investigate these cases personally. He painstakingly sought to determine whether the witness was prone to hallucinations, or whether she might be mistaken about the day on which she had her experience. His fieldwork findings were consistent with the witness's testimony.

Most of these early crisis apparition cases were less than dramatic. This peculiar banality impressed the S.P.R. researchers, since it was out of keeping with the intense drama that typified fictional ghost stories. In fact, one early reviewer of the S.P.R.'s work suggested that these stories tended to put one to sleep rather than banishing it! For example, the following case was reported by a puzzled teacher:

> About fourteen years ago, about 3 o'clock one summer's afternoon, I was passing in front of Trinity Church, Upper King Street, Leicester, when I saw on the opposite side of the street a very old playmate, whom, having left the town to learn some business, I had for some time lost sight of. I thought it odd he took no notice of me; and while following him with my eyes, deliberating whether I should accost him or not, I called after him by name, and was somewhat surprised at not being able to follow him any further, or to say into which house he had gone, for I felt persuaded he had gone into one. The next week I was informed of his somewhat sudden death at Burton-on-Trent, at about the time I felt certain he was passing in front of me. What struck me most at the time was that he should take no notice of me, and that he should go along so noiselessly and should disappear

so suddenly, but that it was E.P. I had seen I never for one moment doubted. I have always looked upon this as a hallucination, but why it should have occurred at that particular time, and to me, I could never make out.

Follow-up interviews substantiated that the witness had never experienced a previous hallucination. The S.P.R. also learned that the witness first told the story to his mother before hearing of the death. The witness's mother unfortunately died before the S.P.R. conducted its inquiry, so this important testimony was lost to them. Nonetheless, the S.P.R. researchers were able to unearth several cases where such testimony was still available to them. In some cases the apparition was even seen by more than just one person, as in the following example:

Some years since, when living at Woolstone Lodge, Woolstone, Berks, of which parish and church, etc., etc., my husband was clerk in Holy Orders, I left the fireside family party one evening after tea, to see if our German *bonne* could manage a little wild Cornish girl to prepare her school-room for the morning. As I reached the top of the stairs a lady passed me who had some time left us. She was in black silk with a muslin 'cloud' over her head and shoulders, but her silk rustled. I could just have a glance only of her face. She glided fast and noiselessly (but for the silk) past me, and was lost down two steps at the end of a long passage that led only into my private boudoir, and had no other exit. I had barely exclaimed 'Oh, Caroline', when I felt she was something unnatural, and rushed down to the drawing-room again, and sinking on my knees by my husband's side, fainted, and it was with difficulty I was restored to myself again. The next morning, I saw they rather joked me at first; but it afterwards came out that the little nursery girl, while cleaning her grate, had been so frightened by the same appearance, 'a lady sitting near her, in black, with white all over her head and shoulders, and her hands crossed on her bosom', that *nothing* would induce her to go into the room again; and they had been afraid to tell me over night of this confirmation of the appearance, thinking it would shake my nerves still more than it had done.

As chance would have it, many of our neighbours called on us the next morning — Mr Tufnell, of Uffington, near Faringdon, Archdeacon Berens, Mr Atkins, and others. All seemed most interested, and Mr Tufnell would not be content without noting down particulars in his own pocket-book, and making me promise to write for inquiries that very night, for my cousin, Mrs Henry Gibbs. She had been staying with us some time previously for a few days, and I had a letter half written to her in the paper case.

I wrote immediately to my uncle (the Rev. C. Crawley, of Hartpury, near Gloucester,) and aunt, and recounted all that had happened. By return of post, 'Caroline is very ill at Belmont' (their family place then), 'and not expected to live'; and die she did on the *very day* or evening she paid me that

Edmund Gurney of the Society for Psychical Research played a leading role in gathering evidence for apparitions. (Mary Evans Picture Library)

visit. The shock had been over-much for a not very strong person, and I was one of the very few members of the Drawley or Gibbs family who could not follow the funeral.

Luckily, one of the independent witnesses was still alive and was able to confirm the entire series of events for the S.P.R.

The fact that apparitional appearances seemed to be genuine paranormal phenomena intrigued the S.P.R. founders no end. Did these appearances, they wondered, constitute evidence that man possesses a soul released from the body at death? This seemed a tenable position to take at first; but when they started examining their data in more depth, they gradually became less sure.

A prolonged debate about the nature of apparitions came to the forefront of psychical research when Edmund Gurney, F. W. H. Myers and their colleague Frank Podmore joined forces to write their two-volume study, *Phantasms of the Living*. This publication was the first major undertaking of the S.P.R. and it was clear that these brilliant researchers could not agree about the nature of phantasms . . . much less whether they represented the release of the soul from the body.

Edmund Gurney wrote the bulk of *Phantasms*. Since he was fascinated by the subject of telepathy, he couldn't shake the idea that apparitions actually resulted from a form of thought-transference. He pointed out that apparitions seem little different in essence from the visual images some people 'see' during the reception of a telepathic message. This led him to suggest that apparitions are merely a more perfectly exteriorized form of mental image. This was a radical stand to take, but Gurney supported his view on empirical as well as theoretical grounds. He pointed out that apparitions do not appear to be objective, space-occupying entities. His data indicated that they never leave anything behind, they appear and then vanish without a trace, can walk through walls, and usually appear dressed in ordinary clothing. These seem to be tell-tale marks of immateriality. Sometimes, Gurney went on to show, apparitions appear dressed in ways the witnesses might *expect* to see them. This would indicate that the figures were partially constructed from the witnesses' own minds.

This was not the last word on the subject of apparitions by any means, since F. W. H. Myers was fast to counter his colleague. He objected that the existence of collectively seen apparitions demonstrated their partial objective reality. His theory was that an apparition results when some aspect of the dying person's organism projects over space and exteriorizes at the distant location. What manifests might therefore not be purely physical in the objective sense, but would represent a partial psychic invasion of its place of manifestation.

Edmund Gurney couldn't go along with Myers' complicated rehabilitation of the idea that apparitions are objective phenomena. So he countered by suggesting that collectively seen apparitions occur through a form of telepathic infection between (or among) the witnesses.

While these debates bandied back and forth, other S.P.R. researchers organized an attempt to replicate the *Phantasms* study. This was undertaken in 1889 by surveying the British public about their psychic experiences, and the results were published in 1894 as the 'Census of Hallucinations'. Reports of crisis apparitions were once again conspicuous by their presence. The evidence for some of these cases was even better than for those appearing in *Phantasms*.

Despite the discovery of so many new cases, it seemed that the debate over the nature of apparitional appearances was heading towards a stalemate. This state of affairs led some of the S.P.R. researchers to study post-mortem apparitions; i.e. those phantoms seen long after the agents' deaths. Through these studies the S.P.R. uncovered cases where the apparitions appeared and even conveyed correct information to the witnesses. In other cases it seemed that the phantoms were interested in fulfilling some goal or intention that had consumed them in life. A few cases of conventional haunted houses also came to the S.P.R.'s attention as well. These cases turned out to be much rarer than crisis apparitions, and some of S.P.R. leaders were rather dubious about their value. F. W. H. Myers studied them the most intensely and soon concluded that they represented '. . . manifestation of persistent personal energy', but he was sharply criticized by Frank Podmore. Podmore, who eventually became the S.P.R.'s resident sceptic, pointed out that most post-mortem apparitions rarely displayed any true sense of personality. He preferred to believe that these accounts were either bogus, or that the apparitions were created by the witnesses' own minds, although perhaps in response to the reception of psychic information.[3]

Mediumship and the Case for Survival

The S.P.R.'s great debate over the nature of apparitions occupied the attention of the Cambridge group from the 1880s well into the 1890s. While an a priori case for survival could be built on their data, these case studies certainly did not constitute the type of hard evidence for immortality for which they were searching. So they began looking in different directions for this evidence. It was by way of this expanded approach to the survival issue that the S.P.R. founders were led back to the spiritualist movement, despite their distaste for the fraud they knew was rife within its ranks. The founders of the S.P.R. had all investigated spiritualist mediums during their early studies, and they were ambivalent about their findings. They were encouraged, however, when William James, the brilliant and esteemed Harvard psychologist/philosopher, contacted them in 1885 with stunning news: he claimed to have found a genuine trance medium through whom he had spoken with his own, purportedly deceased, relatives.

Testimony from such a critically minded source couldn't be ignored, and a new chapter in parapsychology's search for proof was about to open.

Mrs Leonore Piper wasn't exactly the picture of a spiritualist wonder-worker. She was a middle-class and married Bostonian who had lived an eminently normal life. Her introduction to the spiritualist movement came only after she suffered some medical problems as a result of an accident. Her father-in-law suggested that she see a prominent blind clairvoyant in Boston to hear what he would have to say about possible treatment. It was during her first consultation that something strange occurred. Mrs Piper later explained that as she sat listening to the psychic, 'his face seemed to become smaller and smaller, receding as it were into the distance, until gradually I lost consciousness of my surroundings.' She had apparently entered into a spontaneous trance, which surprised her since she had previously entertained no interest in spiritualism.[4] She started attending some of Dr Cocke's regular seances anyway, and soon discovered that she, too, had trance ability. It wasn't long before she was the talk of the spiritualist community, since during her trances her clients seemed capable of making contact with their deceased friends and relatives.

Mrs Piper was only 25 years old at the time and her burgeoning mediumship probably wouldn't have come to scientific attention at all were it not for a fortunate development. William James's mother-in-law heard about her, visited the young psychic, and was so impressed by her performance that she guided James's attention to her. James and his wife sat with Mrs Piper shortly thereafter and were astounded by the accurate messages they received.

James attended several sittings with Mrs Piper from 1885 to 1886, and several of the incidents he witnessed especially impressed him. During one sitting, for example, the psychologist and his brother were told that their aunt (who was living in New York) had just died that very morning at 12.30. James knew nothing of the matter, but as he later wrote, 'On reaching home an hour later I found a telegram as follows — Aunt Kate passed away a few minutes after midnight.'

The S.P.R. was naturally impressed by stories such as these, so in 1887 they decided to take action. They sent one of their most critical investigators to Boston to look into the case and report back to them.

Mrs Leonore Piper was the 'one white crow' who proved spirit communication to William James' satisfaction. (Mary Evans Picture Library)

Richard Hodgson was a keen and rigidly sceptical investigator, but he was also passionately devoted to psychical research. He set sail for Boston and ended up spending the next eighteen years of his life studying Mrs Piper's mediumship.

Richard Hodgson came to the United States in part to take over the reins of the American branch of the S.P.R., which William James had helped to organize. His first major project was to take complete charge of the Piper case. His plan was to book her sittings himself, study her background, and make sure she wasn't secretly studying her sitters. He even had her trailed by detectives. He also insisted that many of the sitters he booked remain anonymous to her. Despite these formidable controls, the quality of the Piper mediumship remained impressive. She would merely sit down with the client, suffer some minor convulsions and enter a trance, and soon a curious personality who called himself 'Dr Phinuit' would speak through her and act as master-of-ceremonies for the session. Hodgson was never much impressed by Dr Phinuit since the persona's French was practically non-existent and he could never give a very credible account of his terrestrial life. Phinuit actually seemed to be a split-off portion of Mrs Piper's own mind, or so Hodgson argued. But despite his dubious credentials, Dr Phinuit was often brilliant at bringing through veridical messages from the dead.

Hodgson later reported that at his first sitting at Mrs Piper's home, Dr Phinuit successfully described and helped bring through some of his own departed friends. The control especially mentioned an old school friend and called him by his proper name. 'He says you went to school together,' he explained to Hodgson. 'He goes on jumping-frogs and laughs. He says he used to get the better of you. He had convulsions before his death struggles. He went off into a sort of spasm. You were not there.'

All of this rather trivial information was correct, and it alerted Dr Hodgson to the fact that he was being confronted by a case of epoch-making potential.

The communications that followed the appearance of his old friend impressed him even more. Hodgson was from Australia and many years before his move to England he had fallen in love with a young woman. Marriage never entered his life, however, and the woman passed on long before the time of the present sittings. Hodgson was astounded when Phinuit began describing the young woman, and she was able to bring through several deeply personal messages which, more than anything else, convinced Hodgson of the authenticity of the Piper mediumship.

Despite the startling nature of the evidence, Dr Hodgson was not sure that he was actually making contact with the dead. It was true that the messages seemed to be coming from the world of the dead, and he spent months supervising the sittings of other clients whose personal experiences were leading them to the same view. Yet like so many of S.P.R. founders, Hodgson found himself grappling with the same old telepathy versus spirit communication debate that was plaguing the study of apparitions. It was certainly reasonable to assume that Mrs Piper's messages came from the dead; but it was also possible that she was reading the minds of the sitters and gathering up all the pertinent information. He reasoned that this information could then be used to help build up perfect (but bogus) personations of the dead. This line of reasoning was tempting since Mrs Piper's chief control actually seemed to be bogus. It didn't take too much of a leap in faith and logic to assume that *all* the spirits that regularly came through her also had their psychological roots within her own mind. Hodgson at first actively favoured this view, which he put forth in his first major paper on the case.[5]

He was not the only person to receive such evidential messages, since many of the sitters he booked in Boston reported similar success. So in order to test Mrs Piper under even more stringent conditions, Hodgson and his colleagues decided that she should go to England and sit for the S.P.R. leaders in person. They would then be in a position to supervise her closely for themselves. The trip would also allow the researchers to be sure that Mrs Piper was not secretly learning about her sitters' backgrounds, since she had never visited England before, and could not have had access to information about them. The sitters in this case were, of course, the researchers themselves.

Mrs Piper sailed for England in 1889 and was met at the docks by F. W. H. Myers and Oliver Lodge, an influential physicist at the University of Liverpool and one of the S.P.R.'s leading lights. They carefully controlled every move she made and even, with her consent, opened her mail to make sure no one was 'feeding' her information. Despite these incumbrances, she gave seances for the S.P.R. both in Liverpool and Cambridge with outstanding success.

It would be impossible to go into great detail about these important sittings. Lodge was perhaps the most impressed with Mrs Piper, partly due to his own experiences with her.[6] The following is a report Lodge filed about a single incident that occurred during one of his first sittings. Remember that this is actually just one episode which occurred during a more lengthy session:

It happens that an uncle of mine in London, now quite an old man, and one of a surviving three out of a very large family, had a twin brother who died some twenty or more years ago. I interested him generally in the subject, and wrote to ask if he would lend me some relic of his brother. By morning post on a certain day I received a curious old gold watch, which this brother had worn and been fond of; and that same morning, no one in the house having seen it or knowing anything about it, I handed it to Mrs Piper when in a state of trance.

I was told almost immediately that it had belonged to one of my uncles — one that had been very fond of Uncle Robert, the name of the survivor — that the watch was now in possession of this same Uncle Robert, with whom he was anxious to communicate. After some difficulty and many wrong attempts Dr Phinuit caught the name, Jerry, short for Jeremiah, and said emphatically, as if a third person was speaking, 'This is my watch, and Robert is my brother, and I am here. Uncle Jerry, my watch.' . . .

Having thus ostensibly got into communication through some means or other with what purported to be a deceased relative, whom I had indeed known slightly in his later years of blindness, but of whose early life I knew nothing, I pointed out to him that to make Uncle Robert aware of his presence it would be well to recall trivial details of their boyhood, all of which I would faithfully report.

He quite caught the idea, and proceeded during several successive sittings ostensibly to instruct Dr Phinuit to mention a number of little things such as would enable his brother to recognise him . . .

'Uncle Jerry' recalled episodes such as swimming the creek when they were boys together, and running some risk of getting drowned; killing a cat in Smith's field; the possession of a small rifle, and of a long peculiar skin, like a snake-skin, which he thought was not in the possession of Uncle Robert.

All these facts have been more or less completely verified.

The only problem with evidence such as this is that Mrs Piper liked to hold the hands of her sitters. It was suggested by some sceptics that somehow the sitter might be communicating information to the psychic by making unconscious and subtle muscular movements. This idea was especially championed by Andrew Lang, an early S.P.R. member and a pioneering anthropologist and folklorist. He engaged Lodge in a prolonged debate over this issue in the S.P.R.'s publications. Lang was sceptical of Mrs Piper, but even he finally admitted that the 'snake-skin' reference cited above was just too good to be dismissed.

Several of the Society's leaders were able to work with Mrs Piper during her trip. They filed a joint report on their work with her in which they came to four main conclusions: (1) that there was no reason to suspect Mrs Piper's good faith or honesty, (2) that Dr Phinuit was probably a secondary personality of the psychic's own mind, (3) that he often 'faked' his way through some of the sittings, but that (4) on a good day he could bring through voluminous amounts of highly evidential material. The S.P.R. researchers would not, however, commit themselves as to whether these messages emanated from the dead. This was an issue on which they were hopelessly divided. Sir Oliver Lodge preferred this theory to any other about the source of Mrs Piper's communications, but the telepathic hypothesis loomed far and wide and some researchers favoured it.

Even though the S.P.R. could not agree about the source of Mrs Piper's communications, its leaders did not cease studying her formidable abilities. She returned to Boston in 1890 where she once again worked under Hodgson's auspices. Although the reasons were not clear, it now seemed that the quality of her mediumship was improving. Some of her sittings were so impressive that the telepathic hypothesis had to be stretched widely to account for them. This was certainly the opinion of the Revd and Mrs S. W. Sutton, who first attended sittings with Mrs Piper in 1893.[7] Their hope was to establish communication with their little daughter Katherine, who had died only six weeks before. The Suttons were intelligent people and they brought along a note-taker supplied by Dr Hodgson, so today we still have a complete stenographic record of what transpired during their critical sitting of 8 December. This was an occasion on which several departed members of the Sutton family spoke through Mrs Piper, including their daughter. The sitting is so crucial to understanding the psychology of the Piper mediumship that an edited version of the sitting is transcribed below.

This seance began as Mrs Piper took hold of the note-taker's hands. Her trance followed in short order and then Mrs Sutton took the psychic's hands in her own. It didn't take the enigmatic Dr Phinuit very long before he was able to bring through her daughter. He almost began the sitting with the words, 'A little child is coming through.' The Suttons could then hear the control coaxing the child to come to him, and he spoke as if *he* were their daughter. This was typical of the control, who often proxied in this manner. He reached for a medal and a band of buttons that the Suttons had placed on the seance table, and then spoke:

Dr Phinuit	Mrs Sutton's Annotations
I want this — I want to bite it. Quick, I want to put them in my mouth . . .	She used to bite it. The buttons also. To bite the buttons was forbidden. He exactly imitated her arch manner.
I will get her talk to you in a minute. Who is Frank in the body? . . .	We do not know. My uncle Frank died a few years before. We were much attached. Possibly Phinuit was confused and my uncle was trying to communicate.

A lady is here who passed out of the body with tumour in the bowels . . .

My friend, Mrs C. died of ovarian tumour.

She has the child . . . She is bringing it to me. Who is Dodo? Speak to me quickly. I want you to call Dodo. Tell Dodo I am happy. Cry for me no more. [Phinuit puts his hands to his throat.] No more sore throat any more. Papa, speak to me. Can not you see me? I am not dead, I am living. I am happy with Grandma. [Phinuit now speaks for himself:] Here are two more. One, two, three here . . . one older and one younger than Kakie. That is a boy. The one that came first. The little one calls the lady, Auntie. I wish you could see these children. [Addressing Mr Sutton, to whom he turns:] You do a great deal of good in the body. [To Mrs Sutton:] He is a dear man. Was this little one's tongue very dry? She keeps showing me her tongue. Her name is Katherine. She calls herself Kakie. She passed out last. Tell Dodo Kakie is in spiritual body. Where is horsey? Big horsey, not this little one. Dear Papa, take me wide [to ride]. [Speaking for Katherine:] Do you see Kakie? The pretty white flowers you put on me I have here. I took their little souls out and keep them with me. Papa, want to wide horsey. Every day I go to see horsey. I like that horsey. I go to wide. I am with you every day . . .

The name for her brother George.

She had pain and distress of the throat and tongue.

My mother had been dead many years.

Correct.
Both were boys.

Not her aunt.

Her tongue was paralysed, and she suffered much with it to the end.

Correct

I gave her a little horse.
Probably refers to a toy cart and horse she used to like.

Phinuit describes lilies of the valley, which were the flowers we placed on her casket.
She pleaded this all through her illness.

I was so hot, my head was so hot.

I asked if she remembered anything after she was brought downstairs.
Correct.

Some further messages were received and Kakie referred to her sister Eleanor by name. Then, to the Sutton's great surprise, the communicator began singing a song that was sung to her before she died. The little communicator urged her parents to sing along with her, and the couple complied. While they were singing, they could hear a soft, childlike voice coming out of the psychic's mouth and intoning the precise words with them. Two stanzas were sung before the sitting could progress. Then the child sang yet another song she had known in life through the entranced medium. It actually seemed as if the child was talking directly through Mrs Piper and was no longer using the control as a proxy. What so impressed the Suttons was that these two songs were the *only* two the child knew completely. Phinuit seemed to re-insert himself at this point, and the sitting continued:

Dr Phinuit

Where is Dinah? I want Dinah.

I want Bagie.
I want Bagie to bring me my Dinah. I want to go to Bagie. I want Bagie. I see Bagie all the time. Tell Dodo when you see him that I love him. Dear Dodo. He used to march with me. He put me way up.

Dodo did sing to me. That was a horrid body. I have a pretty body now. Tell Grandma I love her. I want her to know I live. Grandma does know it, Marmie — Great — grandma, Marmie.

Mrs Sutton's Annotations

Dinah was an old black rag-doll, not with us.

Her name for her sister Margaret.

Correct.

We called her Great Grandmother *Marmie,* but *she* always called her *Grammie.* Both Grandmother and Great Grandmother were then living.

With evidence such as this pouring in, Dr Hodgson found himself doubting the idea that telepathy could explain Mrs Piper's utterances. Even the somewhat questionable but crudely lovable Dr Phinuit began proving himself a bit. But it wasn't until one of Hodgson's own friends died and began communicating through Mrs Piper that he finally changed his entire verdict about the Piper mediumship. This new development came in 1892 during a crucial stage in the mediumship.

Before 1892 the Piper mediumship was characterized by two features. She always delivered her messages by trance speech and her transition to the trance state was accompanied by fits and spasms. This was the stage of the mediumship dominated by Dr Phinuit's ever-present personality, much to the chagrin of those researchers who considered him nothing but a sub-personality of the medium's. But in 1892 Mrs Piper began developing (under Hodgson's guidance) automatic writing which soon superseded the trance speech. The transition to the trance state also became gentler and more facile during this period. The real change in the trance state came, however, with the appearance of a new trance-personality who replaced Dr Phinuit as the psychic's primary control. George Pellew (whom Hodgson called 'George Pelham' throughout his writings on the case) was a young and philosophically minded friend of the researcher's. He had sat with Mrs Piper himself once before his death and long remained intrigued with the problems of trance mediumship. His death came in 1892 as a result of an accident, and it wasn't long before he started communicating through Mrs Piper. He soon took control of the Piper trance state altogether.

The appearance of the Pelham control also heralded a new dimension in the quality of the mediumship. It became more focused and consistently evidential. Hodgson also used the Pelham persona to test the possible spiritistic basis of the entire mediumship. During the next several months, he introduced 150 sitters to the seances, of whom 30 had known Pelham during his life. The Pelham control was able to accurately recognize 29 of them. His only lapse came when he failed to recognize a young woman he had only known as a child. Most of the sitters were able to talk and reminisce with the Pelham personality as though he were right there in the flesh, and the quality of his many trance conversations was certainly equal to that of the Sutton sittings. Hodgson was so impressed by this new personality that he issued another report on Mrs Piper in 1898 in which he outlined his reasons for converting to the spiritistic theory.[8]

The subsequent history of the Piper mediumship is no less imposing or dramatic. She underwent several more changes in control, and when Dr Hodgson died suddenly in 1905, he subsequently communicated through her. Mrs Piper's mediumship began to deteriorate in 1911 and she lost her trance state altogether, though the automatic writing continued for several more years. She held sittings well into the 1920s and died in 1950.

Perhaps it seems by now that the entire case for survival could be based on the Piper mediumship. Even with such high evidential quality, though, some of the S.P.R. old guard were still sceptical of the spiritistic hypothesis. For example, several of her 'communicators' still turned out to be fictional characters and even the most credible communicators

— who should have known better — supported the legitimacy of the blatantly fictitious ones. Even the highly regarded Pelham personality could not discuss philosophical issues very well through Mrs Piper, despite the fact that the subject was very close to his heart when he was alive. It was in hopes of clarifying some of these problems that the S.P.R. was always on the lookout for new and gifted trance mediums. This development was certainly fortuitous in one respect, since many of the original S.P.R. founders were beginning to pass on. It was now up to a second generation of researchers to continue with their work.

The Cross-Correspondences

F. W. H. Myers died in 1901, which was one year after the death of Professor Henry Sidgwick. Gurney's death had come, tragically, by possible suicide some years before. The S.P.R. leadership now fell into the hands of a team of new intellects headed by Alice Johnson, who was a protegé of Professor Sidgwick's wife, and J. G. Piddington, a scholar and barrister who soon devoted his full attention to psychical research. These researchers threw themselves into the study of the Piper mediumship, but they also began working with several other trance psychics who appeared on the scene. Chief among these were Mrs Margaret Verrall, the wife of a Cambridge professor of classics, and her own daughter Helen. Both of them were well aware of the S.P.R.'s work before they actually developed their own mediumships. The S.P.R. also found itself studying the automatic writings of Rudyard Kipling's sister in India, whom they identified only as 'Mrs Holland' in their reports on her. She actually contacted *them* when she found herself suddenly receiving automatic writings from the surviving F. W. H. Myers! The last of this group of new trance mediums was a woman only called 'Mrs Willett' in the reports and who was one of the most talented of the group. It wasn't until years after her death that her identify was revealed as Mrs Winifred Coombe-Tenant, a prominent British stateswoman of the time. It was extremely lucky that the S.P.R. was able to find so many talented mediums, for it appeared that the deceased founders of the Society were themselves eager to establish communications from beyond the veil.

That these eminent scholars should seek to contact their colleagues is not surprising, but what *was* surprising was the nature of their communications. Sometimes one of the psychics, working alone at home, would scribble a message that made little sense, but which seemed to relate to what one of the others was writing at about the same time. These messages often seemed to be coming from the deceased Myers. Piddington and Johnson realized very quickly that curious jig-saw puzzles were being communicated through the scripts; for when the messages

Mrs Margaret Verrall was the protagonist of the 'cross correspondences' which she felt were the deliberate handiwork of a single personality, that of the recently deceased F. W. H. Myers. (Mary Evans Picture Library)

were joined together, an important communication would be spelled out. These puzzles were immediately called the 'cross-correspondences' and represent a very important chapter in the literature on trance mediumship. They went on for years, and it appeared as though Myers was devising his own very personal way of proving his continued survival to the colleagues he had left behind.[9]

Some of the cross-correspondences became enormously complex, since Myers was in the habit of drawing his material and citations from classical Greek and Latin literature. Most of the mediums were ignorant of this body of literature, but Myers was an authority on it, so his choice was certainly *a propos*. One of the easier cases to follow is the case of the Medici tombs, which the soi-disant Myers communicated through several S.P.R. sensitives in 1906. The cross-correspondence first came to light when Mrs Holland was visiting England that year. Some of her private scripts of that period contained messages from Myers alluding to death, sleep, shadows, dawn, evening and morning. No clues to the meaning of these themes were given except that the name 'Margaret' (Verrall) was appended.

Such cryptic allusions immediately suggested that a cross-correspondence case was in the works; so upon learning about the scripts, Alice Johnson and Piddington started checking the writings their other psychics were producing and sending to them. Since Mrs Piper was also visiting England at this same time, J. G. Piddington sat with her a few months later and she spoke the following words while emerging from trance: 'Morehead — laurel for laurel. I say give her that for laurel. Goodbye.' She also saw the apparition of a negro. This really didn't make all that much sense either, so Piddington held another session with Mrs Piper the very next day. During this seance Myers communicated directly and explained that the key to the cryptic message could be found by examining Mrs Verrall's scripts. (Remember that this same message was alluded to in Mrs Holland's germinal scripts). It turned out that the discarnate Myers was a little off the mark, for the next allusions to the puzzle came in Helen Verrall's scripts written in Cambridge. She followed up on the laurel theme by writing one day: 'Alexander's tomb — laurel leaves, are emblems, laurels for the victor's brow.' Mrs Holland was also still under the influence of the alleged Myers, for shortly after the Verrall scripts arrived, she found herself writing one evening: 'Darkness, light, shadow, Alexander Moor's head.' It should be noted that none of the psychics was in contact with any of the others.

There seems little doubt but that these messages were all interrelated, though they probably will make little sense to the modern reader. But the S.P.R. leaders were versed in classical literature and history, and the

F. W. H. Myers with his son Harold. (Mary Evans Picture Library)

allusions made considerable sense to them. The final key came when Mrs Willett contacted the S.P.R. with some of her own automatic writings, which contained the words: 'Laurential tomb, Dawn and Twilight'.

It was now apparent that all these messages referred to the tombs of the Medici family in Italy. J. G. Piddington explains in his report on this cross-correspondence that the laurel was the family emblem of Lorenzo the Magnificent, a one-time patriarch of the Medicis. Other symbols carved on the family tombs represent dawn and twilight. The allusion to Alexander was not too puzzling either, since Alessandro de Medici had been another member of the family. He was known as 'The Moor' because of his mulatto heritage, and he was secretly buried in the Medici tombs.

One interpretation of this case, then, is that the deceased Myers used his knowledge of the tombs to inject a literary jig-saw puzzle into the scripts of the mediums. This was the type of information with which Myers was well conversant, but which was beyond the education of some of the psychics.

The case of the Medici tombs is actually a rather simple and compact one. Some of the other cross-correspondences were much more complex and took years to complete. The pinnacle of the cross-correspondences probably came in 1906 when Mrs Piper was still in England. During one of his sittings with her, Piddington delivered a specially constructed message to the purported Myers which set the stage for it. He explained to 'Myers' through Mrs Piper: 'We are aware of the scheme of the cross-correspondences which you are transmitting through various mediums; and we hope that you will go on with them. Try to give to A and B two different messages, between which no connection is discernible. Then as soon as possible give to C a third message that will reveal the hidden suggestions'. He also proposed that Myers designate his allusions to the cross-correspondence by signing the pertinent scripts with a triangle transcribed within a circle.

Now there was an important catch to this message, for *it was read to the entranced medium in Ciceronian Latin*. Mrs Piper, of course, understood no Latin and especially not such an obscure dialect, but the language was well within the command of the living Myers. Mrs Piper's controls responded to the message by saying they understood.

It took only a few weeks for the deceased Myers to spell out this complicated cross-correspondence. Between 17 December and 2 January allusions of the themes of stars, hope, and the poetry of Robert Browning started cropping up in the writings of Mrs Verrall and her daughter. These allusions made little sense to Piddington until he received a message at a sitting with Mrs Piper in London to 'look out for Hope, Star, and Browning'. The allusions then all made sense when Piddington read up on Browning and found that the cross-correspondence related to themes contained in his poem *Abt Vogler.*

The cross-correspondences went on for years, and gradually began ebbing in the 1910s. The S.P.R. leaders found them very convincing evidence for survival, although they tend to be very problematic for the modern student. The greatest difficulty with the cross-correspondences was that it took a great deal of classical scholarship to fully appreciate them. Writing in 1972, Dr Robert Thouless — a British psychologist and an authority on the survival problem — went so far as to suggest that, 'if this was an experiment devised . . . on the other side of the grave, I think it must be judged to be a badly designed experiment. It has provided a mass of material of which it is very difficult to judge the evidential value, and about which there are varying opinions.'[10]

Dr Thouless's verdict is a little harsh, but it echoes the sentiments of many contemporary researchers. It is nonetheless important to note that those researchers who studied the cross-correspondences most intensely came to see them as strong and almost irrefutable evidence for life after death. The only exception was the always sceptical Frank Podmore, who believed that telepathy among the sensitives could explain them. He especially focused on Mrs Verrall as the source of the leakage, since she alone among the psychics had a good background in the classics.

New Developments in Research on Mediumship

The decline of the Piper mediumship and the cross-correspondences in general after 1910 or so did not impede the progress of survival research in Great Britain, however. It merely closed one chapter in the search while opening up yet others. Psychical researchers were becoming more sophisticated by this time and they were beginning to realize that they needed new ways of exploring the nature of trance mediumship. That chance came in 1915 when Sir Oliver Lodge brought the S.P.R.'s attention to yet another great medium. She was a native born Englishwoman who sported a trance guide name 'Feda', who in turn claimed to be from India where she had died as a child. Unlikely it may have sounded, but research with this talented trance medium would occupy organized psychical research for the next two decades and beyond.

Mrs Gladys Osborne Leonard was born in 1882. She experienced visions and paranormal encounters as a child, but like so many other psychics her mediumship didn't blossom until she started experimenting with table-tilting, in the basement of a theatre where she was working as an actress. Trance followed and by 1915 she was becoming prominent in London spiritualist circles. A friend of Sir Oliver Lodge and his wife attended one of her sittings that year and were impressed enough to recommend her to the physicist. Lodge sat with her after learning about her talents, and he and his wife received a number of evidential communications from their son, who had been killed in the war. The most impressive piece of evidence was a detailed description of a photograph which the communicator claimed had been taken of himself with his platoon. This photograph arrived in the mail some time after the sitting.[11]

Mrs Gladys Osborne Leonard who gave more than seventy sittings which convinced the S.P.R. that her psychic abilities were genuine (Mary Evans Picture Library)

Lodge was thoroughly acquainted with the psychology of mediumship through his long association with the Piper work, but it fell to new and more innovative researchers to explore the possibilities offered by the Leonard mediumship.

Probably the most celebrated series of experiments made with Mrs Leonard was undertaken by Ann Radclyffe-Hall, the celebrated novelist then serving on the S.P.R.'s council, and Una, Lady Troubridge in 1919. The main communicator during these sittings was a deceased friend of Miss Radclyffe-Hall, referred to only by her initials (A.V.B.) in the reports. [12] The two investigators had their first sitting with Mrs Leonard at her home on 19 August, during which Feda described a woman about 60 years old who wished to communicate. She also described the woman's facial features and the way she wore her hair. These were clues that allowed Miss Radclyffe-Hall to identify the communicator, since her friend had only recently died, at the age of 57. The A.V.B. persona also communicated at the next sitting, at which time Feda explained how the communicator 'looks sideways at people sometimes, without moving her head, she's looking at you like that now.' This was all very characteristic of the living Miss A.V.B., and the description impressed the sitters.

Perhaps the most critical sitting of the series was held on 22 November. The communicator used this occasion to deliver a group of evidential messages about a trip to the Canary Islands which she and Miss Radclyffe-Hall had once undertaken. The persona described the scenes of their adventures together, and finally mentioned which islands they visited. To quote from the records of the sitting:

Feda	Do you know anything about an island, that is not far from there?
M.R.H.	Yes, I do know something about an island.
Feda	She suddenly said: 'Island, island, island', she keeps on showing Feda a piece of land standing in the middle of water, and she says:. 'It's a piece of land standing in water.'
M.R.H.	Yes, it is an island.
Feda	She says that place is called Ter — ter — terra — Oh! Feda can't quite get it, but she wants to say that it's a place called Ter — Te — no, Feda can't get it, but it starts Te. It's Tener — Tener — Ten — Ten — What, Lady? Tener —
M.R.H.	Tener is right.
Feda	Teneri — Teneri — ee — ee — ff — ffe — ife — Teneri-fer. She says she doesn't agree with the 'fer' she says Tener is right, she says cut off the last 'er' and it's right.
Feda	(Sotto voce: Tenerife, it's Tenerife!) She keeps on saying an island, it's an island she says, and she says it's a nice place, she says: 'Tenerife!' Do you know, she pushed that through suddenly? She pretended

that she was exasperated at your not understanding. She thought that Feda would get hold of it if she pretended to be cross. Now, she's saying that there's that place called M. again. — Masager — Masager — Madaga — Maza.

M.R.H.   Maza is right, Feda.

Feda   Mazaga — Mazager — Mazagi — Mazagon — (We here omit several other efforts on Feda's part to pronounce the name, which efforts end with *Mazagal.*)

M.R.H.   No, not quite Mazagal, Feda.

Feda   Mazagan!

M.R.H.   That's right, Feda.

Mazagan was the name of a city in Morocco the two women had visited en route to the Canary Islands.

During a later sitting, Miss Radclyffe-Hall put a 'test' question to the communicator. She asked Feda (through the entranced sensitive) whether the communicator could remember the word 'poon'. Feda immediately responded that the communicator was laughing and replying that the word was used to express a state or condition. This correct response encouraged the sitter to ask the communicator to cite the other word they had once coined. Feda seemed to have difficulty receiving the word from the entity, so the matter was dropped for the moment. But at the next sitting Feda suddenly interrupted her line of thought to exclaim, 'Sporkish! Sporkish. She says its the antithesis to poon.'

This was correct. The two women had invented these words as a private code to designate those people whose dispositions they liked or found annoying.

The sittings undertaken by Miss Radclyffe-Hall and Una, Lady Troubridge to contact Miss A.V.B. lasted for two years. The communicator even developed the ability to control the medium directly, who often spoke with the same vocal characteristics typical of the woman's speech in life. This dramatic aspect of the Leonard mediumship was not isolated to this one case, since many other sitters during these years found their deceased relatives directly controlling the trance. Mrs Leonard's whole demeanour would change on these occasions, and she would take on the vocal and even the physical characteristics of the communicators. These verisimilitudes were extremely impressive to many of the sitters.

Despite the fact that the Radclyffe-Hall reports were extremely evidential, they really contributed little to the survival question. Despite the very dramatic quality of the Leonard mediumship and the evidence, the sceptics still maintained that the crucial information could have been telepathically derived from the sitters' own minds. It was obvious that a fresh approach to the study of mediumship was needed, and it came about when C. Drayton Thomas, a British clergyman and an active S.P.R. member, started working with Mrs Leonard in 1917. He sat regularly with the psychic at her home in London and received rather voluminous messages from his departed father and sister. Drayton Thomas also instituted a peculiar sort of test with his father's entity, which became known as 'book tests', and which opened a new chapter in the search for evidence for psychic survival.[13] For these experiments, Drayton Thomas would ask the communicator to psychically scan books either in a sealed package or at home in his own library. The idea was to force the communicator to offer information that couldn't be stolen from the sitter's own mind.

These experiments worked extremely well. One of the most dramatic tests of this kind came during one of Drayton Thomas's first sittings with Mrs Leonard. He explains in his report how he was sitting at home one night when he heard some peculiar 'raps' in the house. His first thought was that these might be attempts on the part of his father to establish psychic contact with him. He attended a sitting with Mrs Leonard soon after where he learned more about the mystery. Feda — without any prompting on the sitter's part — spontaneously alluded to the incident and claimed that *she* was the one who had rapped in the clergyman's house. Feda then brought through Drayton Thomas's father, who communicated a rather cryptic message through Feda's proxy. The communicator instructed his son to return home and find a volume '. . . behind your study door, the second shelf from the ground, and fifth book from the left. Near the top of page 17 you will see words which seem to indicate what Feda was attempting to do when knocking in your room.' The communicator added, 'Now that you are aware that it is Feda's attempt you will see the unmistakable bearing of these words upon it.'

The clergyman could hardly wait to get home in order to see if Feda and his father were correct. The book designated at the sitting turned out to be a volume of Shakespeare. The page indicated contained a most appropriate passage from *King Henry IV* which read, 'I will not answer thee with words, but blows.'

Successes such as these were numerous and their accuracy could not be explained away as the result of coincidence. In fact, some of the S.P.R. researchers — spurred on by Drayton Thomas's successes — conducted mock book tests among themselves and came up with practically no success. Drayton Thomas later expanded these experiments by having his father's persona predict words and passages that would appear in the next day's newspapers. These experiments, too, were highly successful.

The results certainly indicated that Mrs Leonard possessed extraordinary psychic ability. Drayton Thomas also succeeded in demonstrating that simple telepathy could not account for much of the information his father's revenant was communicating. He therefore favoured a spiritistic interpretation of the communications. But looking back on all these experiments today from a more modern perspective, Drayton Thomas's opinion seems a little flawed. Researchers during these critical years did not, unfortunately, realize that a psychic could rely on clairvoyance and precognition just as easily as on telepathy. So the contemporary sceptic could easily argue that Mrs Leonard merely used her own psychic powers to read the books and newspapers, and then placed the information in the mouths of her ('self-proclaimed') communicators.

This type of theorizing is difficult to refute, but it doesn't explain the curious psychology of the book-tests. Drayton Thomas was able to show that his father's persona achieved his greatest successes when alluding to books that had been his personal favourites in life. This discovery seems much more consistent with the spiritistic theory. If Mrs Leonard were relying on her own psychic powers during the tests, she should have been equally successful with any of the volumes.

The Revd C. Drayton Thomas went on to explore several other aspects of the Leonard mediumship. He finally came to the conclusion that the best way to test the mediumship was by separating the sitter from the actual sessions completely. This led him to implement what he called 'proxy sittings', in which he would sit with the sensitive in the client's absence. He would merely show up for the appointment and explain to Feda that he was sitting for an absent party who wished to make contact with a specific communicator. His hope was that Feda would be able to bring through the desired individual even under these stringent conditions. The combined results of the many proxy sittings undertaken by Drayton Thomas, and later by Sir Oliver Lodge's secretary, demonstrated that the procedure did not impair the results. The most celebrated of these many proxy sittings was reported by the S.P.R. in 1935, and concerned a series of seances the clergyman held on behalf of a stranger who had written to him. The gentleman wished to contact his deceased grandson, who had died only a month before.

Drayton Thomas was at first sceptical, since he didn't think that such a young communicator could manage to speak through the sensitive. His doubts were quickly dispelled. 'Bobbie Newlove' was able to communicate with the help of the psychic's controls, and took little time sending a series of veridical messages to his grandfather. Included among these messages was the correct description of a dog-shaped salt-shaker he owned in life, a sandwich-poster costume he once wore, and even the name of the street that bordered his school. The most provocative message the boy communicated concerned some pipes located in a field near his school, where he liked to play. These pipes were eventually located and it seemed likely that the boy fell ill after drinking the stagnant water dripping from them.

Towards the end of her mediumship, Mrs Leonard finally developed what might be considered the ultimate proof of survival. The sitters could hear a third voice speaking in the seance room, which often whispered information to Feda (who was directly controlling the medium's normal speech). This voice was sometimes quite loud and was often caught by the tape recorder, a new mechanical contrivance of the day, that was used to make permanent records of the Leonard mediumship. The tapes I have personally heard are extremely impressive since the 'direct voice' is loud and clear and definitely that of a man. (These tapes were made during some of Drayton Thomas's sittings and the direct voice is purportedly that of his father.) The voice sometimes sounds just as if there were a third person in the room, and it talks frequently and boldly throughout the session.

Mrs Leonard continued to give sittings into the 1940s. Her death came in 1968.

Despite all the evidence, no final solution to the survival problem ever evolved from the study of mediumship. The lure of the telepathic hypothesis soon became reincarnated as the 'super-ESP' theory — which argued that a psychic could use unlimited powers of telepathy and clairvoyance to build up his or her secondary personalities into spiritistic personations. Something akin to the super-ESP hypothesis was even partially demonstrated in 1921 when S. G. Soal, a noted British psychic investigator, undertook a series of seances with Mrs Blanche Cooper at the British College of Psychic Science in London. He was able to establish contact with an old school acquaintance named Gordon Davis who communicated a number of evidential messages. The evidence for spirit communication was impressive, but it later turned out that the communicator was still alive. Subsequent research revealed that the psychic had described details of the house into which this gentleman only moved after the sittings were completed.*

---

*Since S. G. Soal later falsified the results of some of his ESP tests at the University of London, some researchers are sceptical of all his claims and reports. However, there is some independent evidence that the Gordon Davis communications were received just as Soal recorded them. Gordon Davis also testified to the truth of the whole matter up until his death in the 1960s. It should also be noted that the other cases of spirit communicators who later turned up alive and well can be found in the literature.

By the 1930s survival research was becoming more and more frustrating. But the lack of finding definite proof for life after death was not the primary reason why the field left the survival issue behind to go on to other areas of research. Despite its emphasis on the survival problem, psychical research was also devoted to the study of extrasensory perception. Experimental research into the phenomena of telepathy, clairvoyance and precognition came to the forefront of parapsychology at this time. These years saw the emergence of the parapsychology programme at Duke University in Durham, North Carolina, where J. B. Rhine caused a stir in the scientific establishment with his new discoveries. By using simple statistical procedures, Rhine showed that many people could out-guess the laws of chance by 'calling' the order of geometric symbols stamped on cards. His data and approaches revolutionized the entire field. ESP testing soon became the rage at many American colleges and universities, and some of the younger guard at the S.P.R. even left the seance room for the safer confines of the laboratory. Parapsychology would never be the same.

Despite the fact that experimental research is currently at the forefront of parapsychology, this does not indicate that the survival issue should be considered a permanently 'shelved' issue. On the contrary, survival research has been making a slow but sure comeback since the 1970s. The renaissance of interest in the issue was, no doubt, sparked by the initial research that emerged from the Kidd legacy, described in the next chapter. Looking back over parapsychology's first century, it is clear that great gains were made in the study of the survival question. The first psychical researchers demonstrated that the issue of human immortality could be scientifically and critically explored. They also demonstrated that certain forms of psychic phenomena bore directly on the question. These phenomena — primarily apparitions and trance mediumship — could be used to build a legitimate *a priori* case for survival.

There were only two catches. First, the founders of the S.P.R. found that exploring the survival problem was infinitely more complicated than they had imagined. They also failed to form a consensus on the criteria by which the survival issue could be authoritatively resolved.

Today, one hundred years after the birth of psychical research, parapsychologists find themselves still grappling with these same issues. So when the survival problem became of interest to research workers beginning in the 1970s, they found themselves exploring new directions in their search for evidence of man's immortality.

2.

Mind Out of Body

The following account was written in 1965 by a teenager from California:

> One day during the summer of 1965, I came home from summer school as usual, plopped down on my bed, and kicked off my shoes. It was one of those blistering hot days when even the flies don't bother to buzz about, and I just wanted to snooze for awhile. But as I lay there, a funny feeling came over me. I realized that I couldn't move and that my whole body was throbbing as though I was being charged by an electrical current. Then I began to feel as though I was floating. I closed my eyes, in order to 'flow' with the experience, and within a couple of seconds I found myself floating above my own body. I could see it clearly, though everything in the room seemed shrouded in a pink mist. No sooner did I realize that I was literally 'out of my body' than I found myself standing next to my bed. I tried to walk to the door, but I never made it. I wobbled about a bit and, moments later, found myself back on the bed.

At the time, the young man thought that he had just undergone a truly unique experience. He was wrong, since literally thousands of people have had this same type of experience. Some undergo it while ill or by coming close to death, while others encounter it as a result of falling off a bike, getting hit by a car, or other life-threatening accidents. On the other hand, a few people (such as the teenager quoted above) have had the experience without any catalyst at all. It just 'happened' to them, usually while they were resting or relaxing. But it is an experience that most people, once they have it, swear they will never forget. Recent polls indicate that the majority of people who experience this disembodied state find it pleasurable and would like to have another. It is also a very common experience and polls recently conducted both in the United States and England indicate that one out of every five people will have one sometime during his or her lifetime. Few people, however, ever seem able to actually develop the ability to 'leave the body' at will.

These people do exist, nonetheless, and over the last few years several top parapsychologists have seen actively inviting them to prove their claims in the laboratory.

When Dr Gardner Murphy addressed the Arizona court litigating the Kidd case on 6 June 1967, he brought up the subject of the out-of-body experience. 'These are experiences', he explained, 'lasting ordinarily a few minutes, sometimes hours, in which the person, usually in a sleeping or a comatose state, appears to himself to wander forth from his body, takes up his station perhaps miles away from where his body is, and may look back and see the house in which his body lies . . . '

The psychologist added that 'under some conditions the individual is actually seen by others. There are a few cases in which the experience involved visibility to another individual who sees the person, not in terms of where his body is back in the sick bed, but where he is out enjoying the open air.' Dr Murphy was intrigued by these reports. He suggested that if the out-of-body presence could produce some sort of material effect at its point of projection, such a phenomenon could help resolve the survival problem. It would demonstrate that we possess some aspect of 'mind' that is capable of leaving the body and existing apart from it.

This view has long been espoused by supporters of the survival theory. It seems logical to conclude that if the mind can function away from

The astral body leaving the physical body, based on Sylvan Muldoon's accounts of his out-of-body experiences. (Mary Evans Picture Library)

the body for a limited time, it might be able to function independently of it *permanently*. This is why some researchers interested in the out-of-body experience maintain that the study of this phenomenon is critical to the survival problem. The data presented in the last chapter demonstrated the immense difficulty of ever proving that the dead can directly contact the living. The OBE holds out the promise that the survival issue might be resolved by showing that we, the living, possess an *innate* capacity for surviving the shock of death.

This is why research on the nature of the out-of-body experience has become crucial to the survival issue. The key issues at stake are simply: Is the OBE a 'genuine' form of psychic phenomenon? And if so, does anything truly objective or detectable actually leave the body during the experience? Proving either of these possibilities would automatically lend support to the idea that the OBE is, in fact, an experience we will eventually use to transcend death.

Experimenting with the Out-of-Body Experience

Parapsychologists have been interested in the out-of-body experience since the time of F. W. H. Myers, but it has only been fairly recently that attention has been devoted to exploring its parameters. The topic never became a focal point of serious research endeavour because it didn't quite fit into the 'hard' look parapsychology adopted in the 1930s.

Experimental research into the by-ways of the OBE had its beginning in France at the close of the nineteenth century. Researchers there induced OBEs in their experimental subjects through hypnosis and tried to get their liberated 'astral' bodies to produce raps or influence delicate scales. They even attempted to photograph the human 'double'. Considerable success was reported, but it is very difficult to evaluate this research today. The first attempts to study the OBE scientifically in more contemporary times came only in 1965 when Dr Charles Tart, a psychologist at the University of California at Davis, turned his attention to the subject. His interest was aroused when a young woman contacted him with the claim that she was experiencing OBEs nightly. Tart's response was to suggest that she cut up some slips of paper, write numbers on them, place them in a box, shuffle them, and then, — before going to bed — pick one of them without looking at it and place it somewhere in the room out of her sight. Tart explained to her that, in order to prove the reality of her experiences, she should try to view the number while out-of-body. She could then evaluate how accurate her out-of-body vision was, thereby possibly documenting the experience.

When the woman reported back to him a few days later that she had been successful, Dr Tart was even more intrigued. He was soon able to recruit her for a series of tests at his sleep laboratory at the university.[2]

The experiments were quite simple. Each night for four days, Miss Z (as Dr Tart identified her in his report) would come to the lab and try to sleep there. The lab room was outfitted with a cot where Miss Z would lie after being hooked up to electrodes. These led to a polygraph which monitored her brain waves and other physiological responses as she slept. A ledge extended from the wall above the cot, and each night a paper with a five-digit number was placed there by the psychologist. Miss Z was simply instructed to go to sleep and, should she find herself out-of-body during the night, float up and memorize it. An intercom connected the sleep chamber to an adjacent equipment room where a researcher monitored the experiment, so that she could communicate the number immediately.

Nothing very exciting happened during the subject's first three nights, but the fourth session was amazingly successful. Shortly after six in the morning, the subject called out over the intercom. She reported that she had just been out-of-body and recited the number to the experimenter. She gave all five digits correctly. Even more suggestive was what her brain waves were showing at the critical time. The EEG readings demonstrated that, just before calling out over the intercom, Miss Z slipped from normal sleep into a rather strange and unclassifiable 'drowsy' state that didn't represent clear-cut sleeping or waking. This suggested to Dr Tart that something more than simple ESP had been involved in his subject's success.

It was later learned that the number on the ledge could have been seen by shining a flashlight near it and catching sight of its reflection on a clock located above it. But there was no evidence to assume that the subject knew about this flaw, or smuggled a flashlight in the lab, and it is probable that any major movement on her part would upset the electrodes attached to her body.

Parapsychologists in general took little notice of Dr Tart's work, which was formally reported in 1968. But when the Kidd money was awarded to the A.S.P.R. (and subsequently to the P.R.F.), researchers at the two organizations began to reconsider the OBE. Perhaps following up on Dr Murphy's suggestions, they felt that approaching the survival problem by working with the *living* might be more fruitful than expanding on the old mediumistic approaches. Their focus turned towards demonstrating that we possess the capacity to survive, not whether contact with the dead can be established directly.

The result of this thinking was that, for the next few years, both organizations would devote considerable time, energy, and money to exploring the OBE. Their goal was to work out a way to demonstrate that some aspect of the mind really leaves the body during the out-of-body experience. Since such a finding might be considered a 'proof' of the soul, the research was certainly well within the spirit (excuse the pun) of the Kidd will.

Explorations into the Nature of Out-of-body Vision

Research on the OBE was spearheaded at the A.S.P.R. by Dr Karlis Osis, the organization's long-time research director. Dr Osis had previously been interested in the survival problem and the Kidd money gave him just the opportunity he needed to devote his full time to it. After reading up on the OBE, he decided that the best way to approach the problem was by exploring the nature of out-of-body vision. He reasoned that OBE 'sight' should conform to the principles that govern physical vision, which is very unlike the vague and fragmented way ESP messages are received and processed. He hoped to show that a psychic undergoing an OBE would be able to 'see' or 'view' much more consistently than an ESP subject might be expected to perform. He also expected that OBE 'sight' would be *limited* by the same factors that interfere with normal vision.

Luckily, Dr Osis didn't have long to wait before he was able to test his ideas. His chance came when he began experimenting with Ingo Swann, one of the more colourful practitioners on the psychic scene and a long-time resident of New York.

Ingo Swann is a well-built, blondish, cigar-smoking former United Nations worker who soon became one of the most talked about psychics in the country. He is also a professional artist. He first discovered he could leave his body when he was a child having his tonsils removed. Years later as a young adult, he learned to control this very special talent. He found that he could not only project an element of his mind completely away from his body, but could remain perfectly conscious at the same time. So to induce his OBEs, Swann merely sits in a comfortable easy-chair, usually puffing away on his cigar, 'liberates' part of his mind and then casually tells the experimenter what he is 'seeing' while his mind is floating about.

An entire series of OBE experiments was carried out with Swann by Dr Osis and his associate, Janet Mitchell, at the American Society for Psychical Research in 1972.[3]

For their first tests together, a room at the A.S.P.R. headquarters was specially prepared. Swann was seated in an easy-chair, hooked up to a polygraph, and asked to project his mind to the ceiling and 'look' at a platform-like box suspended from it. Two target pictures were placed next to each other in the box, and Swann was requested to look at one, describe it, and then 'swing around' the platform and look at the other

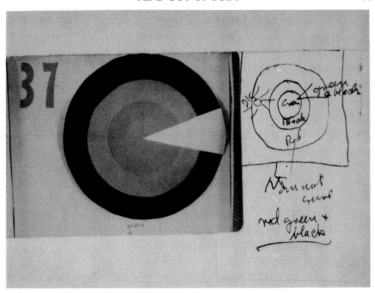

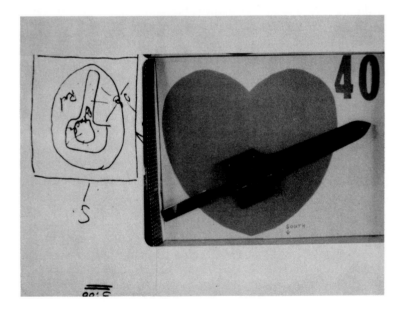

American psychic Ingo Swann scored dramatic successes by 'visiting' the targets (on left) in an 'out-of-body journey', then sketching what he had seen (right). (Mary Evans Picture Library)

picture. Later he was asked to sketch what he had seen. Several trials were made using this same procedure, but different targets were supplied for each test.

It isn't hard to discern the rationale behind these tests. If three objects were placed next to each other on the platform, Osis wanted to know whether Swann would see all of them and in proper perspective to one another. If he could, Osis believed that this would indicate that the OBE is a phenomenon very unlike normal telepathy or clairvoyance, since these faculties are rarely very precise. It would, instead, demonstrate that something really does 'leave the body' during the experience.

To say the least, Swann performed sensationally. For one trial, both pictures were composed of geometrical forms. One was an inverted red heart with a black letter-opener case laid over it, while the other was a tri-coloured bull's-eye with a pie-slice cut out of it. While out-of-body, Swann was able to see and later draw both of these targets precisely. He didn't confuse one with the other. His sketch of the bull's-eye was so uncannily accurate that he even placed the pie-shaped slice in the correct position. He made only one error, by reversing the colours of the rings composing the bull's-eye. For the heart and letter-opener case, he drew an egg-shaped oval with an oblong knife-like object on top of it. He also correctly designated their colours.

Swann was also capable of coming up with a few surprises of his own during these experiments. Osis and his co-workers soon learned that Swann's OBE vision could become so unnervingly accurate that he was sometimes able to perceive aspects of the targets that even *they* were unaware of. Swann describes one of these incidents in his autobiographical book, *To Kiss Earth Good-Bye:*[4]

> During the experiment of March 3, when the box enclosure was carefully lined inside with white paper, the person constructing the target inadvertently did not cover some printing on the inner side. This printing was 'seen', but not read, by me as I tried nervously to perceive what was in the box. After the experiment was completed, but before the box had been taken down and inspected, the person who had structured the target got excited and indicated that this trial must have been a 'flunk' since there was no printing in the box. Bristling, I indicated that I had, nonetheless, perceived printing there, and so it must be there. To everyone's chagrin, when the box was taken down and inspected, there was the printing, just as I felt I had seen.

To test the relationship between OBE vision and physical sight even further, Osis developed a new test for his potential OBE subjects to try their hands (or minds!) at. Once again he hoped to show that 'something' actually leaves the body during the experience. With the help of some of his collaborators, he developed what he called the 'optical viewing box'. This device looked just like a simple black box mounted on a stand. It measured three feet high by two feet wide, and a curious hole was opened right in the middle of it. A person looking into the box would see a wheel divided into four differently coloured segments. A slide projector was also rigged up to the box which, when activated, seemed to throw any one of several pictures onto a selected quadrant. I say 'seemed to project' because the super-imposition of the picture on the wheel was actually an optical illusion.

This optical illusion was actually the key to the whole test. Osis believed that a psychic, looking through the hole in the box while out-of-body, should be able to correctly see the optical illusion — just as you or I would if we looked into the box with our physical eyes. He further believed that a subject merely using clairvoyance to 'scan' the box psychically would probably not perceive the illusion at all.

To test out his magic box, Osis recruited another psychic as his new guinea-pig.[5] Alex Tanous is a mysterious-looking, dark-eyed, ex-theology professor from Maine and he became Osis's second star OBE subject. Unlike Swann though, Tanous actually claims to project a phantom-like image of himself during his OBEs. He also claims that this 'double' has been seen occasionally by people to whom he has projected.

In order to test Tanuous's self-proclaimed OBE talents, Osis stationed the Maine psychic in one room at A.S.P.R. headquarters across the corridor from the room in which the optical box was situated. The psychic was merely instructed to sit or lie down, project himself to the box, look in, and then report which picture he saw and in which quadrant he saw it projected.

Tanous at first totally failed at the box test, much to Osis's disappointment, but it was Tanous himself who worked out what the problem was:[6] 'When I first began working with the optical box,' he later recalled, 'I couldn't see the target image because I wasn't tall enough — at least my other self wasn't tall enough. The window on the front of the optical box is about eye level for a person of medium height. My projected self, my astral body, as I see it, has hardly any height at all. It's a small ball of light. I couldn't see into the window unless I strained, unless I "stood on tip toes" — even then, I couldn't see well.'

Dr Osis had his assistant build a platform for Tanous' parasomatic body to stand upon and, sure enough, the psychic suddenly became more successful at seeing into the box!

Experiments to Detect the Out-of-Body Self

While all this work was being undertaken in New York, research into the mysteries of the out-of-body experience was also being pursued down south in North Carolina. Research there, however, soon began moving in very different directions from that at the A.S.P.R. During the 1970s, the Psychical Research Foundation was a small and under-funded organization housed in two small wooden buildings next to Duke University. Despite its unpretentious trappings, the P.R.F. ultimately spent two years engaged in epoch-making research exploring the nature of the out-of-body experience. What is also so amazing is that P.R.F. researchers focused their attention on only one experimental subject.

Keith 'Blue' Harary originally found his way to the P.R.F. in 1973.[7] He had just enrolled at Duke University as an undergraduate when he learned that the P.R.F. was looking for people who believed that they could voluntarily leave their bodies. Since he had been having the experience ever since he was a child, he eagerly offered his services. His claim that he could *voluntarily* leave his body sparked the immediate interest of the P.R.F. staff! So the project was quickly turned over to Dr Robert Morris, then the Foundation's director of research. It was Morris's plan to see, of course, if Blue really could leave his body as he said.

For the first phase of his experiments, Morris asked Blue to remain in one P.R.F. office building while their co-workers hung large cardboard letters on a door or wall in the other house some twenty yards away. Blue's job was to leave his body, visit the other building, and then report on what he had seen there. In order to make his psychic voyages, Blue would simply lie down, relax, and allow his mind to leave his body. He usually induced the experience from a sealed booth, since he didn't like being watched as he tried to send his mind away from his body. In order to keep in constant contact with the experimenters, though, Blue would signal Morris over an intercom when he felt he was about to leave his body. He would then give another signal a few minutes later when he returned. Immediately after he had adjusted himself back in the body, Morris would ask Blue to report what he had seen while making his psychic journey.

Several of these 'target' studies were run, and Blue had varying degrees of success with them, and it soon became clear to the P.R.F. workers that the OBE was not a simple cut and dried matter. Sometimes Blue was almost stunningly accurate at describing the posterboard letters, while at other times he failed miserably. However, the P.R.F. staff also learned that Blue had a psychic trick or two of his own up his sleeve.

For instance, during one test the only person who was supposed to be in the building with the posterboard letters was Joseph Janis, one of the P.R.F. staff members. Unbeknown to Blue, however, another experimenter — a volunteer named Jerry Posner — had entered the room

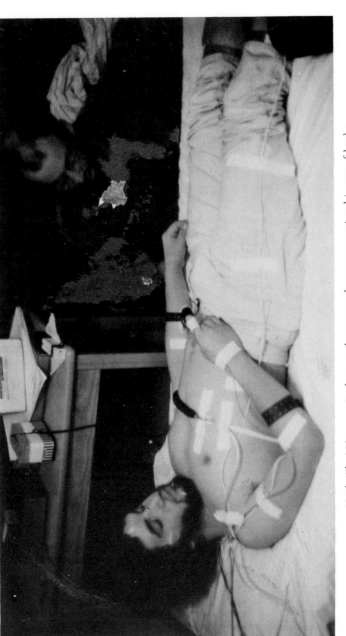

Keith 'Blue' Harary wired up so that researchers can monitor his out-of-body attempts. (Mary Evans Picture Library)

during the test to keep Joe company. Although Blue failed to see the target letter accurately during the experiment, he immediately picked up the presence of the second person in the room and reported it to Dr Morris.

By no means was this the end of this unusual story though. After the experiment was over, Posner claimed that he had actually *seen* Blue's apparition in the room with him! The time Posner saw the apparition closely corresponded to the time Blue was making his out-of-body attempt. This unexpected incident alerted the staff to the fact that Blue might be better able to respond to people than to cardboard letters. It also gave them the idea for their next experiments with him.

For this new series of tests, four P.R.F. staff members were instructed to sit in the Foundation's meditation centre for the entire time of the experiment. This centre was a small building directly behind the two P.R.F. office buildings across a grass quad. Blue was then taken to another building, placed in a small sealed booth, and asked to shoot over to the centre, see who was sitting there, and report their names to the experimenters. Blue, of course, was kept in complete ignorance as to which of the dozen or so P.R.F. workers were sitting there. Nonetheless, he scored perfectly on the first test. Not only was he able to accurately report *who* was sitting in the meditation centre, he was even able to correctly tell exactly *where* each volunteer was seated!

Even though his accuracy fell below par over the next few tests, the P.R.F. researchers were rather startled by the fact that, on occasion, some of the people seated in the room seemed to either 'see' Blue's apparition or detect his presence in some other way. The timings of these detections usually tallied with the time Blue was making his OBE attempts. Even Dr Morris had one of them! So instead of solving the OBE mystery, the P.R.F. workers soon found themselves being sucked right into it.

Like so many sensitive people, Blue adores animals. Since he seemed so proficient at making people respond to his out-of-body presence, the P.R.F. staff came up with a wonderful idea for their next major project. If Blue could somehow make human beings react to his presence, they wondered, what about animals? By tradition, animals are supposed to react oddly in a haunted house or when visited by ghosts and their kith and kin. The P.R.F. people naturally wondered how they would react to the presence of a living ghost. So in order to find out, two kittens were less than voluntarily recruited for the test and the next phase of the Harary research was underway. The kittens were appropriately named Spirit and Soul.

For these new tests, Robert Morris employed what is known as an 'animal activity board'. This is simply a shuffleboard-shaped plank which is chequered into several equal squares. By placing an animal on the board, the experimenter can make a record of its basic 'activity rate' by noting how many squares it passes over and how many times it makes a noise during a given period of time. Morris's plan was to see if the cats would react or act differently when Blue mentally visited them than at any random time. The actual experiment was a complex one, though, and only one kitten was used. Here's how it was carried out:

Blue was first taken to an experimental room at Duke University Hospital, which was located about a half mile away from P.R.F. One experimenter stayed with him, while another monitored the kitten based at the P.R.F. lab building. The kitten-watcher was only told that, during the experiment, a phone in the room rould ring four times. Each ring would initiate a two- or three-minute experiment during which time he was to pay close attention to the kitten; but on only two occasions would Blue *actually* project to the animal. During the other two, he would merely think about leaving his body or would do nothing at all. The experimenter stationed with the kitten had, of course, no idea which of the four periods would be the actual times when Blue would be making his attempts. His job was merely to watch the kitten and keep track of its behaviour during these four periods.

This experiment was run several times and the results were simply amazing. The kitten would invariably become very agitated when placed on the board. It would jump about and miaow continually. Yet every time Blue projected to it, the kitten would suddenly calm down, sit motionless, and wouldn't miaow at all. Its change in behaviour was often so striking that the investigator monitoring the kitten had little trouble working out just when Blue was making his visitations.

The 'kitten' experiments were run with different animals as well. I personally arrived in Durham to act as an advisor on this research in the summer of 1973, when the kitten experiments were just being completed. Discussion among the staff was rife about what the next phase in the research should be. There was some talk about using less domesticated animals, since animals normally adapted to a wild habitat would be more vigilant and threatened by an unseen presence. Some of us figured that they might therefore react more strongly to an out-of-body visitor. It didn't take us long to find an appropriate subject for our tests. Mr Graham Watkins, another advisor on the project, was an animal behaviourist with a penchant for snakes. His pride and joy was the nastiest snake I've ever seen. It positively hated people and would never stop striking at any one who dared to come near it. Watkins offered us the loan of it (along with his handling gloves!) for the experiments.

For the first test, a team of researchers took Blue over to Duke Hospital after first synchronizing their watches with me. I remained at the P.R.F. along with a volunteer worker. The building in which we were located contained a small isolation booth complete with an observation window. The snake and its terrarium were placed there while I monitored its behaviour through the window. The experiment was run along similar lines to the kitten sessions. I merely watched the snake and took note of its behaviour while waiting for the lab phone to ring. This would signal a three-minute experimental period. Through the next hour or so, the phone rang four times and Blue tried to project to us twice. We had no idea which of the two periods constituted the true experimental periods.

During the course of the experiment, the snake only made one odd response. Before the test and during the first experimental period, it was as calm as could be and simply meandered about its cage rather undramatically. The snake seemed to become more agitated at the beginning of the second experimental period. To my amazement, it slid up the side of the cage and literally seemed to attack the side of the terrarium. It bit at it wildly and then — just as mysteriously — calmed back down again. The response lasted about twenty or thirty seconds and it was very startling. The snake exhibited no further unusual reactions for the duration of the experiment.

When the P.R.F. researchers brought Blue back to the lab later that night, we compared times. It turned out that Blue's first OB attempt had been made during that critical second period. He explained to us how he simply left his body, found himself with us, tried to attract our attention, and then projected right into the terrarium with the snake. The timings between when Blue would have been with the reptile, and its radical response, was almost exact.

I should add that we attempted to replicate this experiment a few days later, but the snake decided to be rather uncooperative. Before the test even began, it burrowed into the shavings at the bottom of its cage and went to sleep. I couldn't rouse it, so the experiment was a washout.

The experiments I have just described represent only the highlights of several tests which the P.R.F. team designed to explore Blue's OBEs. The crucial issue, of course, was trying to demonstrate that Blue really was 'leaving the body' as he claimed. This was an issue that, even after two years of research, couldn't be resolved to everyone's satisfaction. Dr Robert Morris ultimately remained sceptical about the overall meaning and implications of the research. He felt that it was theoretically possible that the animals and people who detected Blue's presence were responding to psychic (i.e. telepathic or perhaps psychokinetic) messages from him and nothing more. I, on the other hand, couldn't buy this reincarnation of the super-psi theory, since I didn't feel that it could explain the consistency of the kitten's behaviour. The number of impressive visual and subjective detections of Blue's out-of-body presence also seemed inconsistent with the super-psi idea.

There was even suggestive evidence that Blue could create physical effects at the locus of his projections. During one experiment, for example, he approached a thermistor set up in one of the P.R.F. buildings while projecting from the other. He approached it twice and each time the graph showed a temperature 'dip'. Unfortunately, Blue couldn't produce this effect reliably.

So all in all, the P.R.F. work ended up on a note of uncertainty. It certainly appeared that some element of Blue's mind was leaving his body during his OBEs, but none of the experiments constituted 100 per cent proof.

The research undertaken at both the A.S.P.R. and the P.R.F. came to an end about two years after it was initiated. The reasons were simple — the Kidd money ran out and both organizations once again had to start looking for new funding . . . and for new projects that might bring it in. By 1975 formal parapsychological research into the OBE was almost becoming a thing of the past. The researchers had done just about everything they could to isolate the OBE as an objective phenomenon and not merely an ESP-conducive hallucination. Some of their data were consistent with the 'projected mind' theory, but many of the researchers were disappointed by the inconsistency of the results. If someone were really functioning out-of-body, why couldn't the subject *always* make people react to him, or always see the target objects located in distant locations? No one seemed to be coming up with an answer to this nettling question. Luckily, though, research into the nature of the OBE did not end at this time . . . but it did take on vastly new dimensions. This new research did not, however, come out of conventional parapsychology.

3.

Documenting the
Near-Death Experience

When Raymond Moody's little book, *Life after Life,* was published in 1975 no one thought that it would become a bestseller. It was issued by an obscure publisher in Atlanta, Georgia and contained several rather clinically presented firsthand accounts by people who had 'died' but who later revived. Moody's witnesses invariably told how they had left their bodies, survived death, travelled to a strange and wonderful paradise, and had only reluctantly returned to their bodies. It was perhaps this 'optimistic' view of the death experience which overcame the taboo on discussing death and led to the enthusiastic reception of Moody's book and other similiar studies which followed it. Symposia on the subject of near-death encounters have subsequently been presented at the annual conventions of both the Parapsychological Association and the American Psychological Association; and a society of medical men investigating near-death phenomena has even been organized.

Since the publication of Moody's book, hundreds of people have come forward to talk about their own experiences. These cases represent a growing body of evidence implying that the afterlife is only a brief moment away. For example, in the August 1979 issue of *Anabiosis,* the newsletter of the Connecticut-based International Association for Near-Death Studies, a correspondent writes about a typical near-death encounter, or NDE.

The young man reports that he had his NDE as a result of a hideous accident. He was loading groceries into the back of a car when another car crashed into it, pinning him between two vehicles. He was rushed to a hospital and taken to an emergency room where he lost consciousness.

'Sometime later there was a sudden flash of light and I found myself floating just above my physical body,' he writes. 'I could see the surgeons working on me. There was also a nurse seated in front of me, directly above my head. The next sensation I had was when I felt someone place

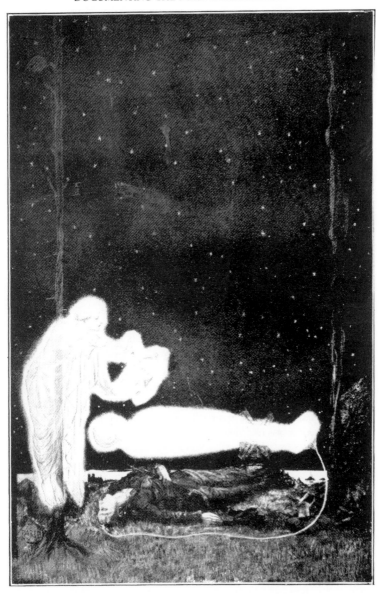

This painting showing man's soul departing his body at the moment of death, executed by G. Parlby under the direction of spiritualist Hewat Mackenzie, shows the 'silver cord' which many experiments have noted. (Mary Evans Picture Library)

their [sic] hands on my shoulders. I got the impression that I was sitting on something which moved me through a tunnel.'

The correspondent went on to explain that he subsequently found himself streaking along the tunnel and coming to rest in a misty environment. He could distinguish people moving about and heard beautiful music cascading about the place. A glowing being finally approached him, questioned him about his life, and then bade him return to his body. He awoke later after returning down the tunnel.

'It was the most beautiful experience of my life,' he later reported.[1] This is a reaction many have after experiencing an NDE.

These types of cases are commanding wide attention. Even the daily papers are reporting them. A case similar to the one cited above was reported in the 30 March 1983 issue of the Los Angeles *Times*, which related the near-death encounter of a young Hollywood businessman.

Dan O'Dowd, the co-owner of a video company in Los Angeles, was nearly killed when he was forced off the Pacific Coast Highway, which runs along the coast of Southern California, by a drunken driver. The date was 27 August 1979. What resulted was a series of fifty operations during which the young executive was slowly pieced back together. His NDE occurred during an especially gruelling fifteen-hour operation at Cedars-Sinai Medical Centre in Beverley Hills. He was lying on the operating table when, he later revealed,

> . . . all of a sudden I went from having the heaviest drugs to put me under to being completely cold sober and seeing the cardiac [monitor] machine going in a straight line. I was totally awake, even though I know my eyes were closed. It was like viewing television pictures. Then I soared up and was looking down on myself. I was a foot-and-a-half to six feet hovering over my body.

He looked on in amazement as one of the attending physicians suddenly announced that he was dead. The executive had apparently had his NDE during a crisis in the surgery.

O'Dowd next found himself in the adjacent hallway where his relatives were assembled and watched incredulously as a doctor came out to tell them that the operation had failed. Soon, though, he found himself back in the operating room where the doctors were still trying to save him, despite their pessimism. As he watched in amazement, they applied defibrillator pads to his body in the hope of shocking his heart back into action. 'One guy grasped those thumpers,' he explained to reporters, 'and someone put some gel on me and I'm looking down and I look terribly dead. Then they put those big shockers on me and blast away.

The first time nothing. The second time it started me back up and immediately I could feel myself being sucked back under the anesthesia. And out.'

The 32-year-old businessman lived to tell the tale. His relatives still remember how the doctors told them that his heart had stopped and that they were doing all they could to save him, though they were doubtful that they could. His doctor, Dr Mohammed Ataik of Cedars-Sinai, also remains puzzled by the incident. 'I do not want to contest him,' he admitted to the *Times*, 'but I have no explanation for it medically.'[2]

Episodes such as these in the face of death are surprisingly common. After studying over a hundred such accounts, Moody has shown that a person undergoing an NDE will experience any number of several prototypical experiences. In the most involved cases the patient or accident victim will commonly experience a moment of peacefulness as he realizes he has died; he will often hear crashing noises; will feel himself 'leaving his body' and journeying towards a brilliant white light, and sometimes he will experience an instantaneous review of his past life before finding himself in the hereafter. At this point the experience usually ends, since the witness either returns to his body automatically, or is told to return by someone he meets in the afterworld.

Many followers of Moody's work believe that cases such as the one quoted above virtually prove that we will ultimately survive death. But the evidence is not that clear-cut. During the last seven years there have been several attempts to discredit Moody's research, while several other scientists have tried to replicate his findings. What has resulted is a scientific controversy almost as fascinating as Moody's original claims. At the present time, researchers have found that the study of the NDE is not as simple and clear-cut as Moody's first enthusiasts considered it to be.

One of the most vocal critics of the life-after-life argument has been Dr Robert Kastenbaum, a psychologist at the University of Massachusetts and the editor of *Omega* — *the journal of death and dying*, one of the most prestigious publications devoted to the psychological study of death. Kastenbaum is personally interested in the evidence for a life after death and even arranged a symposium on the NDE at a recent meeting of the American Psychological Association. However, he has issued several blasts at the life-after-life movement. Writing in the September 1977 issue of *Human Behavior* magazine, Kastenbaum points out that not everyone who has suffered clinical death experiences an NDE. These out-of-body states seem rather infrequent and, argues the psychologist, we therefore have no right to extrapolate from such limited data that the NDE is a universal human experience. He also points out that some people who have had brushes with death often have experiences radically different from the types of NDEs reported by Moody and others. Many people never leave their bodies at the moment of clinical death, but remain consciously *in* their bodies even though they may appear to be in coma or dead.

'The existence of other types of reports from the dead-or-almost-dead frontier does not of itself discredit the kinds of accounts that make up the current wave of interest,' writes Kastenbaum, 'but they do make it difficult to accept the implication, drawn by some, that the process of dying-unto-death is usually a joyous one.' Neither does Dr Kastenbaum believe that these incidents demonstrate the existence of a life after death.[3]

Kastenbaum's opinions have been echoed by other critics who have accused life-after-life devotees of basing their views about the joys of dying on a handful of anecdotal accounts. These critics have also argued that, before Moody's data can be accepted as valid, it would be necessary to poll large groups of people who had come close to death in order to see whether NDEs are common experiences or merely anomalous reports which have occurred to just a handful of people and which have been collected out of context because of their similarity.

Luckily, such objectively conducted surveys have since been carried out. And their results have done much to validate Moody's original findings.

Documenting the Near-Death Experience
One such study was undertaken by Dr Michael Sabom, a cardiologist at the Georgia-based Emory University School of Medicine, and his assistant, Sarah Kreutziger, who in March of 1976 began interviewing people who had experienced clinical death. They eventually spoke to 100 hospital patients, 71 men and 29 women, who had narrowly escaped death. They found that 61 per cent had experienced classical NDEs of the type closely corresponding to those published in 1975 by Moody. These subjects had undergone their NDEs in the face of a variety of mishaps including cardiac arrest, accident, and even suicide.

'The details of these sixty one NDEs were surprisingly consistent,' wrote Sabom and Kreutziger in the 4th quarter 1978 issue of *Theta — a journal for research on the question of survival after death*. 'During the autoscopic experience, all patients noted a "floating" sensation "out of the body" unlike any [they had] felt before. While "detached" from the physical body, the patient observed his or her own body in clear detail.'

Many of Sabom and Kreutziger's cases are virtually identical to the types of experiences reported by Moody. One such report was provided by a security guard who had suffered an anterior myocardial infarction while being treated at a hospital.

'I just couldn't stand the pain any more,' he told the researchers. 'That's when everything went dark and black. After a little while I was . . . floating. I could look down and I had never noticed that the floor was black and white tile. I recognized myself down there, sort of curled around in a half-fetal position.'

The guard then looked on dispassionately as a doctor tried to revive him by electrically stimulating his heart. 'It appeared to me,' he went on to say, 'that I had a choice to re-enter my body and take the chances of them bringing me around or I could just go ahead and die, if I wasn't already dead. I knew I was going to be perfectly safe, whether my body died or not. They thumped me a second time. I re-entered my body just like that.'

The patient never had the experience of seeing a brilliant white light, nor actually travelling to the afterworld. But some of the researchers' other correspondents have.

As a result of their survey, Sabom and Kreutziger have concluded that NDEs are genuine occurrences. They point out that NDE phenomena are very different from the type of hallucinations produced by temporal lobe seizures, drugs, psychological depersonalization (when the subject feels alienated from his body due to stress), or pathological autoscopic ('seeing one's self') hallucinations. What they did find, however, was that people who had undergone NDEs survived the experience with the certainty that they would eventually survive death.[4] But the importance of this research doesn't stop here by any means.

The Study of 'Veridical' Near-Death Encounters

Dr Michael Sabom is now working at the Atlanta Veterans Administration Medical Centre. When he was invited to speak at a special symposium on the NDE at the 1981 annual meeting of the American Psychological Association in Los Angeles, he described the research on which he began focusing after he had completed the research described above. Dr Sabom explained that, while at first he was primarily interested in reports filed by cardiac patients at the hospitals in which he worked, he soon began pursuing reports from other sources. What singularly impressed him as he gathered more and more cases was how some of his cardiac patients and other witnesses actually watched their operations and/or resuscitations during their NDEs. It struck him that many of these informants had seen and accurately described events that were well beyond the medical knowledge of the average layman. Since that time, Dr Sabom has begun publishing several of these cases.[5]

One such report came from a 52-year-old night-watchman from northern Florida. He had chalked up quite a history of heart problems, and was admitted to the University of Florida's medical centre in November 1977 for cardiac catherization and subsequent surgery. Dr Sabom was still in training at the hospital at the time, and was able to do a complete follow-up on the incident. The patient had undergone a prior NDE during a previous operation and experienced a second out-of-body encounter in January of 1978 during his open-heart surgery.

The night-watchman's NDE was fairly typical. He reported initially how he lost consciousness after the anaesthetist inserted an I.V. He explained how he regained consciousness during the operation, but was now viewing the entire proceedings from a point about two feet above his body. That vantage point allowed him to look right down at it and all that was transpiring. He explained the sensation as being 'like I was another person in the room' and watched as the two doctors worked on him and stitched him up after completing the operation. His unique out-of-body perspective also enabled him to make detailed observations of the surgery itself. He saw one of the doctors inject a syringe into his heart on two occasions during the process, each given on either side of the organ. He also noticed that his head was covered by a sheet and was surprised at how dim and diffuse the lighting in the room was.

The watchman was also surprised by the appearance of the heart and how it looked during surgery.

'They had all kinds of intruments stuck in the aperture,' he recalled when Sabom interviewed him . . .

> I think they're called clamps, clamped all over the place. I was amazed that I had thought there would be blood all over the place, but there really wasn't much blood . . . And the heart doesn't look like I thought it did. It's big. And this is after the doctor had taken little pieces of it off. It's not shaped like I thought it would be. My heart was shaped something like the continent of Africa, with it being larger up here and tapered down. Bean-shaped is another way you would describe it. Maybe mine is odd-shaped . . . [The surface was] pinkish and yellow. I thought the yellow area was fat tissue or something. Yuky kind of. One general area to the right or left was darker than the rest instead of all being the same color.

The man soon became engrossed in observing the open-heart surgery, and listened as his doctors discussed the procedures they were contemplating or implementing. They discussed a by-pass, examined an over-swollen vein, and even twisted his heart around to examine it more easily. The patient even noticed that one of the physicians was wearing patent-leather shoes and that another had a small blood-clot under a fingernail.

Dr Sabom was so intrigued by this report and his interview with the man that he dug out the files on the case and read the surgeon's report on the operation. He found that the patient's description represented an amazingly accurate layman's description of procedures actually used during his surgery. A self-retaining retractor had been used, the patient had suffered an aneurysm that had discoloured part of his heart, and the heart had been twisted around during the procedures. Even the syringe that he had seen inserted into his heart had played a role in the operation. It had been used to remove air from his heart . . . and it had been used twice.

What so impressed the Georgia physician was the technical detail included in the man's report. The details he had described didn't seem to be of the type with which an unsophisticated layman would be familiar, and this served as an important clue that the NDE might be representing a more significant phenomenon than most doctors had hitherto considered it to be. Dr Sabom's curiosity was aroused even more when he tracked down the case of a woman in Missouri who had undergone lumbar disc surgery in 1972. She, too, had witnessed her operation while out-of-body and later described it accurately. The catch to this case was that she saw the chief resident participating in the operation, when she had been led to believe that her physician-in-attendance would be playing the crucial role in the surgery. Only later did she find out that the chief resident had directed the surgery, and although she had never met him, she recognized him immediately when she saw him during her recovery.

With cases such as these on file, Dr Sabom soon found himself actively pursuing those reports in which near-death survivors have described the medical procedures used during their operations and resuscitations. These reports have come primarily from cardiac arrest patients, since this is Dr Sabom's own speciality. It is Sabom's belief that, should these observations prove accurate, these very special cases will do much to document the existence, authenticity, and psychic nature of the near-death experience. The cardiologist has now been able to collect some thiry-two cases of individuals who saw their own bodies during their NDEs, and six cardiac arrest victims in particular have recalled specific and accurate details about resuscitations. This is no great number, but the quality of the cases more than makes up for that.

One case that Dr Sabom investigated was contributed by a 60-year-old housewife who had been hospitalized for back strain. She had been sitting in bed when she apparently had a heart-attack and lost consciousness. Regaining consciousness only moments later, she now found herself by the side of her bed and watching the efforts being expended to revive her. A nurse rushed to her inert body, a team of attendants began working on her, began punching her chest, inserted an I.V., gave her an injection, checked for a pulse and examined her eyes. While out-of-body the patient also took a good look at the equipment being used by the attendants. She saw what she called a 'breathing machine' as well as 'a cart with a whole bunch of stuff on it'. This cart stood by the one with the I.V. equipment. She also overheard a doctor tell a nurse that she (the patient) had to be rushed to the intensive care unit, and saw her belongings being taken out of the drawers in the room and stuffed into bags and suitcases.

When Dr Sabom was finally able to interview the woman, he especially concentrated on the patient's description of the equipment cart and asked if the doctors had taken any instruments from it. The woman replied that they hadn't, but added that '. . . the breathing thing they put on my face. It was just a cone-shaped thing that went over my nose. When the doctor was pushing on my chest, they had this on me. They didn't leave it on very long but took it off. I guess they thought it was useless'.

In order to validate the patient's experience, Dr Sabom contacted the hospital where she had been treated and read over the report on the emergency. The records confirmed everything the woman had reported, even though she had never been given access to the hospital report. His conclusion was that her description of the cardiac resuscitation was 'extremely realistic from a medical point of view: the starting of an I.V., external cardiac massage, the administration of oxygen by mask, the checking of carotid pulsations and pupillary response, and the gathering up and labelling of personal effects'. But Sabom didn't stop there. He was also curious about the witness's claim that she had been given an injection right at the start of the CPR attempt. The hospital's medical report documented this procedure as well. The patient had been given an injection of concentrated glucose in case she had fallen into coma as a result of low blood sugar.

Dr Sabom received an even more vivid description of a cardiac arrest resuscitation from a 46-year-old labourer from a small town in Georgia. He had gone into cardiac arrest due to a heart attack he suffered in January 1978. He was hospitalized at the time so he was in a perfect position while undergoing his NDE to observe the steps taken to save his life. Sabom interviewed the witness in January 1979 when the events were still clear in his mind. The patient had vivid memories not only of the NDE but of the events that had led up to it.

'I thought I was getting sick,' he told the cardiologist at the beginning of their conversation. 'I got up on the side of the bed and heaved and that's the last thing I remember until I was floating right up on the ceiling.'

The patient then saw himself lying in bed; the sides were still up. Both his doctor and his wife were in attendance along with a third person he didn't recognize. His wife was crying, but the labourer's attention became quickly focused on the attempts being made to save him. He watched passively as a nurse with a defibrillation machine placed 'them shocker things,' as he called the defibrillator pads, on his body. His body jumped up almost a foot when the electrical charge was sent through it, and the shock aborted his out-of-body experience. It felt as though he were being forced back to his body and pushed inside it.

After receiving this rather brief account, Dr Sabom pressed his informant for more details about the use of the defibrillation pads that had been so instrumental in saving his life. The witness then went on to explain how he had seen the nurse rubbing the pads after first picking them up, and how she had turned on the current by flipping a switch at the right-hand side of the apparatus to which the pads were connected. Everyone had been warned to stand clear, he added.

Once again the hospital records were checked and the accuracy of the patient's report documented. Dr Sabom was especially impressed by the patient's description of the defibrillation pads, since he had described certain procedures associated with their use that only someone with medical training would be familiar with. These pads have lubricant spread over them and are routinely touched together, just as the patient witnessed, in order to spread it evenly over the pads for maximum skin contact. The patient had also correctly designated just where on his body the pads had been placed. Since the patient saw his wife in the room crying, Dr Sabom also interviewed her about the emergency. She verified her husband's account, explaining how she had seen him vomit right before becoming unconscious. She had begun to cry only *after* she thought her husband had lost awareness of what was happening to him.

The patient's wife was really quite flabbergasted by the whole affair — especially when her husband told her what he had seen after he had apparently lost consciousness. His recollections, she told Sabom, matched what she recalled of the scene and the ensuing attempts to save him and get his heart beating again.

Experimenting with the Near-Death Experience
With cases such as these on file, Dr Sabom was becoming more and more convinced that the near-death experience cannot be dismissed as an hallucination or dream. But he was also plagued by one lingering doubt. Could these patients really be *fantasizing* and dreaming about what a cardiac resuscitation might entail on the basis of their prior reading, exposure to television shows, or other sources of CPR information? This was a very real possibility since some of his star witnesses had undergone more than one heart attack. It was Sabom's feeling that they could have

had some exposure to CPR techniques and medical equipment through their prior hospital experiences. Most of his witnesses denied any such knowledge, but Sabom was far from sure that they couldn't have picked up this information quite unconsciously.

In order to investigate this possibility as thoroughly as possible, Dr Sabom conducted a most revealing study. He began to actively interview seasoned cardiac patients about their familiarity with standard CPR techniques. Some of these patients had undergone open-heart surgery, elective cardioversion or heart attacks, which entailed various forms of treatment. So most of them had at least been given the opportunity to observe the use of standard cardiac monitors, defibrillators, and other such equipment. Each patient was asked to imagine that he or she was watching a medical team reviving a heart arrest victim, and to describe in as much detail as possible the steps being taken. These interviews were tape recorded and then analysed.

The results were nothing short of amazing. *Almost all the cardiac patients misdescribed the procedures.*

The most common error was the widespread belief among the patients that mouth-to-mouth resuscitation would be attempted. This, in fact, is rarely used in hospitals since more effective methods of artificial respiration are readily available. The patients also tended to misdescribe how the victim's air passage might be cleared to facilitate breathing, were often confused as to how cardiac massage is implemented, and how electrical defibrillation is discharged. Only three of Sabom's control patients gave reasonably accurate descriptions of some CPR procedures, but even these accounts of the techniques were limited. Dr Sabom concluded from this study that, in general, even seasoned heart patients have little idea just what goes into reviving a cardiac arrest victim. Their conjectures, he noted, were certainly far less accurate than the accounts of those patients who have actually watched these procedures while out-of-body.

As a result, Dr Sabom doesn't think much of the idea that people who have experienced NDEs are only 'dreaming' about their resuscitations on the basis of prior exposure to CPR techniques. 'Some other explanation must be sought to explain these findings,' is his simple conclusion.

The fact that the medical observations made by near-death survivors can be incredibly detailed is demonstrated by one case that Dr Sabom collected from a retired Florida air force pilot. The airman had suffered a massive heart attack one day in 1973 and went into cardiac arrest the next morning while recovering in a hospital. The arrest had apparently occurred while the patient was sleeping. His first memory of the NDE came when he found himself standing to the side of his body. A team of attendants were rushing into the room. His description of how they revived him was full of extraordinary detail.

'The first thing they did,' he reported, 'was to put an injection into the I.V., the rubber gasket they have there for pushes. I was getting a lot of lidocaine all through that thing, lidocaine pushes, 'cause I had an arrhythmia. Then they lifted me up and moved me onto the plywood. That's when [the doctor] began to do the pounding on the chest, and it didn't hurt though it cracked a rib. I felt no pain.'

Next came the administration of oxygen, which the patient heard as well as saw accurately. 'They had oxygen on me before,' he went on to say, 'one of those little nose tubes, and they took that off and put on a face mask which covers your mouth and nose. It was a type of pressure thing. I remember, instead of oxygen just being there, it was hissing like under pressure. Seems like someone was holding that thing most of the time.'

He described it further as 'sort of a soft plastic mask, light green color.' It was attached to a hose leading to the oxygen. He also recalled the use of the defibrillator and how he had watched the meter on it with rapt attention. The meter, he explained, was square with two needles. One was set in a fixed position by the nurse, while the other moved up and down the scale. This second needle 'seemed to come up rather slowly,' he explained as he recalled how he watched the machine being used. 'It didn't just pop up like an ammeter or a voltmeter or something registering.' The other needle remained pre-set all during the CPR attempts. The patient also described how the needle rose higher and higher on the meter before each successive jolt of electricity was applied to his body. He concluded his account by offering a detailed description of the defibrillator itself and the specific methods used when applying its pads to his body.

Not only was the description of the CPR procedures extremely accurate, but the former patient's account of the needles and how they moved was uncannily precise . . . and certainly beyond the learning of anyone who has not had personal experience with a defibrillator or who has never been trained in its use. Those machines used in the 1970s did indeed have two needles on their meters. One remained stable since it was used to pre-select the amount of electricity discharged into the patient. The other needle indicated that the machine was being charged up to the selected amount, and thus it moved gradually up the meter. These machines have now been replaced by more modern models without meters, but the pilot's recollections were totally consistent with the machine that would have been in use at the time of his cardiac arrest.

But could the pilot have actually seen such an instrument in operation at some previous times? The patient denied any familiarity with the apparatus, and Sabom was considerably impressed by how he tended to play-down the importance of his experience. To this day the former cardiac patient insists that there was nothing unusual about it! 'It hasn't changed my thinking about life, death, the hereafter, or anything else,' he told Dr Sabom.

Since the former air force pilot has no vested interest in using his experience to prove anything, it seems unlikely that he would deliberately lie about it in order to make it sound particularly impressive.

The cases briefly summarized in this chapter represent only a few of many similar incidents Dr Sabom has collected. More cases could be cited, some of them in great detail, but they differ very little from those already mentioned above. These incidents all point to the fact that people who undergo NDEs during cardiac arrest — or any other medical emergency for that matter — really are aware of what is happening to them, what procedures are being used to revive them, who is caring for them, and what is being said by the attending medical staff. Subsequent research by Dr Sabom and his colleagues has also demonstrated that the technical level of what they see and hear is well above the elementary level of information most people have about standardly used CPR techniques. There seems little doubt that Dr Sabom's research is probably *the* most important line of evidence that the NDE cannot be dismissed as quirks in the brain, hallucinations resulting from lack of oxygen to the brain, or some obscure psychological anomaly. Dr Sabom also rejects the possibility that these reports can be accounted for as subconscious fabrications, endorphic release in the brain, temporal lobe seizures, or any other physiological cause. All the evidence suggests that these events are just what they are reported to be — the release of awareness from the body resulting from a close brush with death.

So could the NDE actually represent the first stages of the release of the soul from the body?

'As a physician and scientist,' Sabom concludes in his book *Recollections of Death,*

> . . . I cannot, of course, say for sure that the NDE is indicative of what is to come at the moment of *final* bodily death. These experiences were encountered during waning moments of life. Those reporting these experiences were *not brought back from the dead,* but were rescued from a point *very close to death.* Thus, in the strictest sense, these experiences are encounters of *near*-death, and not of death itself. Since I suspect that the NDE is a reflection of a mind-brain split, I cannot help but wonder why such an event should occur at the point of near-death. Could the mind which splits apart from the physical brain be, in essence, the 'soul', which continues

to exist after final bodily death, according to some religious doctrines?

Further Light on the Near-Death Experience

A similar study has recently been undertaken by Dr Kenneth Ring of the University of Connecticut.[6] Over a two-year period, Ring interviewed 102 survivors of near-death brushes. During the course of his work he, like Dr Sabom, also hoped to discover if Moody's data were correct and to see if he could determine whether *how* one almost dies affects the NDE. He initially found that 41 per cent of his respondents had experienced classical NDEs. But he also noted that the content of these NDEs occurred over a progressive *gradient*. Let me explain this a bit. For the purpose of his research, Ring classified the NDE as containing five 'core' elements. These consisted of (1) a feeling of peace at the onset of the encounter, (2) a feeling that one has left the body, (3) entering into a darkness, (4) seeing a light and (5) entering into the light. Ring considered these to be *stages* of the NDE. It was while classifying his NDE accounts according to these stages that he discovered a gradient progression phenomenon. For example, 60 per cent of his witnesses felt a 'peace' at the time of death, while only 40 per cent had out-of-body experiences. And only 10-15 per cent perceived or merged with a brilliant light as they travelled towards the afterlife. This would seem to indicate that the closer one comes to actual death, the more stages one goes through.

Ring has also discovered that there are slight differences between how one experiences the NDE and the way one dies, or whether one will experience an NDE at all. Victims of illness are most likely to have an NDE, while accident victims are next in line. Suicide attempts are the least likely to encourage the manifestation of the NDE. People who have violent near-death encounters are also more likely to experience a 'panoramic life recall'. Ring has also made the fascinating discovery that people who consider themselves religious are no more prone to having NDEs than are agnostics!

Both Drs Ring and Sabom have implied in their writings that the data which they have collected not only support Moody's original findings, but that they demonstrate the likelihood that there is a life after death. This is an astounding conclusion, and it is one which has excited many members of the medical world. Nonetheless, even the careful research of these qualified medical men has not gone unchallenged. There are still several issues which must be resolved before the findings of Ring, Sabom and Moody can be held up as evidence for the existence of an afterlife. Chief among these is that there is no way to determine if the witnesses they interviewed were really dead. It is extremely difficult to isolate the precise moment of death. The fact that people who report NDEs survive their traumas may indicate that they were not really that close to death in the first place. The term 'clinical death' is a somewhat impressionistic one. It is not a precise label. It is usually applied to individuals whose hearts have stopped momentarily during operations or due to heart attacks. But this is a questionable criterion on which to base a diagnosis of 'death.'

A better criterion is through an examination of brain waves. The brain of an individual who has just died does not produce any electrical activity. Such a person, if hooked to an electroencephalograph, would produce no brain waves. Unfortunately, few victims of clinical death have been wired up to an EEG at the time of their traumas.

Critics also pointed out that, as a patient approaches death, it is quite possible that he will suffer *anoxia* — the cutting off of oxygen to the brain. This state may cause hallucinations and could induce the NDE. The experience would therefore be nothing more than a momentary hallucination having nothing to do with life after death.

These two problems — that we don't know whether NDE witnesses were ever really dead, and that their experience may be due to anoxia — are extremely hard to refute. But in May 1979, the International Association for Near-Death Studies announced that they had discovered a doctor in Denver who had collected sufficient data to demolish both of these criticisms! This new evidence indicates that the NDE is indeed a genuine mind-body separation.

Dr Fred Schoonmaker, chief cardiologist at St Luke's Hospital, has been interested in the NDE ever since 1961. It wasn't until 1979, though, that he came forward with his data. In the meantime he had studied well over 1000 cases of clinical death during the course of his practice, and found that 60 per cent of cardiac-arrest-related clinical death patients report NDEs. Although he has not attempted a formal evaluation of his data, and did not follow any scientific protocol while collecting them, Dr Schoonmaker has been carefully collecting as much medical and descriptive information on his cases as possible. These data represent some of the best medical information yet collected on the NDE. In many instances, Schoonmaker's witnesses were being monitored by a host of physiological devices at the time of their NDEs. The Denver physician has collected several accounts of NDEs which occurred at a time when it could be scientifically demonstrated that there was no lack of oxygen travelling to the brain. He has also studied patients who suffered clinical death while being monitored by the EEG, and has collected 55 cases in which patients who have shown 'flat EEGs' (i.e. no electrical activity in the brain) reported NDEs. By all medical criteria, these individuals were irreversibly dead at the time of their experiences.[7]

The Problem of Negative Near-Death Experiences

Though several investigators have now replicated the Moody findings, not all NDE researchers have reported similar data. One near-death investigator who is coming up with very different kinds of reports is Dr Maurice Rawlings, a Tennessee cardiologist, who has collected several NDEs which read quite differently from the peaceful, soothing, transcendental type of episodes reported by Moody, Sabom and Ring. Some of the cardiologist's reports are terrifying NDEs, and these have led Rawlings, as a devout Christian, to believe that they indicate the literal existence of hell.[8]

Rawlings first came across this type of NDE while trying to revive one of his cardiac arrest patients. The patient kept screaming that he was in hell. Since that time, Rawlings has collected many examples of hellish NDEs. For example, one of his correspondents had this type of NDE after a heart attack. As she related to the physician:

> I remember getting short of breath and then I must have blacked out. Then I saw that I was getting out of my body. The next thing I remember was entering this gloomy room where I saw in one of the windows this huge giant with a grotesque face that was watching me. Running around the windowsill were little imps or elves that seemed to be with the giant. The giant beckoned me to come with him. I didn't want to go, but I had to. Outside was darkness, but I could hear people moaning all around me. I could feel things moving about my feet. As we moved on through this tunnel or cave, things were getting worse. I remember I was crying. Then, for some reason the giant turned me loose and sent me back. I felt I was being spared. I don't know why.
>
> Then I remember finding myself back in the hospital bed. The doctor asked me if I had been taking drugs. My description must have sounded like the DTs. I told him I didn't have either of these habits and that the story was true. It has changed my whole life.

In his book, *Beyond Death's Door*, Rawlings reports that one-fifth of the patients he has resuscitated from cardiac arrest report unpleasant NDEs. Many of them forget about their experiences though, he adds. As a result of his personal experience, Rawlings is extremely critical of other life-after-life investigators. He suggests that most people who have had unpleasant NDEs block out the memory of the experience from their minds. Since most NDE investigators only interview near-death witnesses weeks or even months after their clinical deaths, Rawlings believes that their data are biased. He feels that his own data are more objective and complete since, as a practising cardiologist, he was able to collect his cases right after his patients had recovered from their ordeals.

Rawlings in turn has been criticized by other near-death researchers, who have argued that these 'hellish' experiences are really artefacts — hallucinations produced by the witnesses' minds as a reaction to the violent physical ordeals (such as chest poundings and electrical stimulation) which are part and parcel of normal resuscitation techniques.

Nonetheless, Rawlings' data might not be all that easy to dimiss. Dr Charles Garfield, a psychologist at the Cancer Research Institute of the University of California School of Medicine in San Francisco, has also been collecting data indicating that death may not always be a pleasant experience. Dr Garfield has studied 173 terminal cancer patients, some of whom had rather unpleasant experiences while approaching immediate death. While many reported hearing celestial music and seeing a powerful light, others saw demonic figures and nightmarish images. Garfield has also interviewed 72 coronary patients of whom 14 reported Moody-type NDEs, while 8 had 'lucid visions of a demonic or nightmarish nature'. As a result, Garfield has concluded that not everyone experiences a peaceful and transcending death. Unlike many other NDE researchers, however, he does not believe that NDEs necessarily indicate that we will invariably survive death. He feels that they may only be visions which occur when one enters into altered states of consciousness.[9] These mental states might have little to do with the actual physical process of dying.

One cannot help but agree with Dr Garfield that the study of the NDE is in no way a cut-and-dried issue. However, the unpleasant experiences noted by Rawlings and Garfield seem to be anomalous even to their own data collections, besides not being reported at all by other researchers. Nor do they necessarily serve as evidence against belief in life after death. Many spiritual teachers and religions teach that there may be different 'planes' in the afterlife, some of which are more inhospitable than others. Perhaps a few unfortunate people have contacted these 'lower planes', about which such mystics as Emmanuel Swedenborg spoke as far back as the eighteenth century.

What is interesting, though, is that so many men of medicine and science — Garfield is the exception — have come away from their research believing in a life after death, even if they entered the study of near-death phenomena with no disposition to such a view. The study of the NDE may well be the discipline which will finally unite science and religion in a common cause.

4.

Spontaneous Contact
with the Dead

The drama began on 21 February 1977 when the Chicago police found
the body of 48-year-old Teresita Basa. She was lying on the floor of her
fifteenth-floor high-rise apartment stabbed to death and partially burned.
Ms Basa had come to the United States from her native Philippines in
the 1960s, and there seemed little possible motive for the crime. She
worked as a respiratory therapist at Edgewater Hospital on Chicago's
north side and she was popular among her fellow employees. The police
at first felt that her killing may have resulted from a lover's quarrel, but
they withdrew this idea after interviewing her boyfriend. Once again
they were left without so much as a clue.

Teresita Basa's ghost, spirit, revenant, or whatever, was restless, so another
act in the mystery took place four months later at the home of Dr and
Mrs José Chua. Dr Chua was a Philippino physician whose wife had
worked at Edgewater Hospital at the time of the murder. He was surprised
one evening when his wife inexplicably entered a trance-like condition
while they were home together in nearby Skokie, walked to the bedroom,
laid down, and began speaking in her native tongue. 'She spoke in Tagalong
[a Philippine dialect] but with a strange Spanish accent,' he later testified.
'She said 'Ako'y' [I am] Teresita Basa.' The doctor admitted being scared,
especially when Teresita explained that her murderer was another hospital
employee. She accused an orderly named Allan Showery, whose motive
had been the theft of her jewels. Mrs Chua arose from her trance after
the strange voice finished its message, but she remembered nothing about
the brief episode. Dr Chua didn't quite know what to do.

Whatever intelligence was controlling Mrs Chua certainly was persistent.
Another one of these peculiar trances followed a few days later. This
time the voice complained that Showery was still in possession of her
jewels and that he had given her pearl cocktail ring to his common-law
wife. A third communication was received a few days later once again,
after which Dr Chua finally decided to call the police.

The inspectors handling the case, Joseph Stachula and Lee Epplen, were naturally sceptical but were willing to follow up on any lead offered to them. Normal sources of information hadn't given them much to go on, so they met with the Chuas mixing hope with a touch of cynicism. Nonetheless, they went about their work with professional decorum. When they arrived at the Chuas' apartment, they first asked whether 'Teresita Basa' claimed rape as part of the murder. Dr Chua replied negatively and explained that the voice only said that Teresita was murdered. The investigators were impressed by this answer, since their blatantly leading question had been a ploy. They knew from the autopsy report that Ms Basa died a virgin, so it was obvious that the Chuas weren't tailoring their testimony. Then Chuas explained about Showery and the jewels.

'To this day,' Detective Stachula wrote some months later, 'I'm not quite sure that I believe how the information was obtained. Nonetheless, everything [was] completely true.'

True it was. Working from the clues given by Dr Chua and the self-proclaimed ghost of Teresita Basa, the Evanston police began focusing their attention on Showery. A search of his apartment uncovered the jewels and the pearl cocktail ring was found adorning his girlfriend's hand. Showery was arrested, confronted with the evidence, and signed a confession admitting to the theft and murder. The case was officially closed in August.[1]

The strange story of the dead woman who named her own murderer would probably have sunk into obscurity had not the local Philippine press in Chicago caught wind of the story. The *Philippine Herald* ran into a brick wall while trying to get information about the case from the police, but a break came when the paper's managing editor, Gus Bernardes, realized that he knew the Chuas. He was able to dig deeply into the case and eventually learned about several other bizarre psychic twists to the story. He learned, for instance, that several workers at the hospital had complained about Mrs Chua's behaviour during the week preceding the break in the case. She was entering trances at the hospital during which she would sing in Teresita's voice and the episodes had frightened many of the workers. The *Herald* reported the case in their 16 August issue, but the story didn't receive national prominence until 5 March 1978 when the Chicago *Tribune* ran it on its front page. Allan Showery was then coming to trial, which prompted renewed interest in the case. The Chuas' testimony was bound to be brought up, so the sceptics and believers alike were soon having a field day with the story.

The problem was that Mrs Chua had known Ms Basa fairly well . . . at least a lot better than she originally let on to the police. It was also well known that she knew and openly disliked Allan Showery. These new insights led one hospital spokesman to suggest that Mrs Chua's 'spirit voice' messages were ploys she used to express her own suspicions. 'I think she might have known something about Showery but also knew she would be taking chances with her own life and her husband's life if she went directly to the cops; he told the press. He also suggested that Mrs Chua may have seen Showery with some of the jewels.

This theory doesn't explain several curious aspects of the case, however. First was the curious fact that Mrs Chua's whole personality had begun to change sometime prior to when the summer 1977 messages were received. The ordinarily good and mindful employee was even fired from the hospital for insubordination because of the sudden and inexplicable changes in her character which immediately predated the crucial trances. Nor does the spokesman's charges explain why the Chuas simply didn't phone in an anonymous tip to the police. With such a grisly murder on their hands, certainly the police would have acted on any reasonable information. Some further testimony on the psychic aspects of the case came to light in 1979 as well, when the Chuas co-operated in the publication of an obscure little book on the case.[2] They eventually admitted that the summer 1977 trance communications were actually an answer to a challenge. During the investigation immediately following the murder, Mrs Chua once quipped to her fellow hospital employees that Teresita's ghost could come to her if the police failed to catch her murderer. She had seen the woman's apparition a short time later, and the critical trance messages were the outcome of a long-drawn-out invasion of her personality by Teresita.

The case of Teresita Basa's murder and its uncanny dénouement is now closed and only the psychic aspects of it remain controversial.

Cases of murdered victims who return from the grave to name their assailants may sound like the stuff from which campfire-side ghost stories are made. The story of Dr and Mrs Chua and their strange psychic journey seems more like something from Edgar Allan Poe than a case study in psychic research. But the case of Teresita Basa's spirit return isn't unique in the annals of psychic science since similar cases can be dated all the way back to the turn of the century. It played a key role in a West Virginia trial that followed the death of a young bride in 1897. The victim, Zona Heaster Shue, was found dead by her blacksmith husband at the bottom of their home's staircase, and the body was buried quickly without a medical examination. Not everybody was convinced that her death was an accident, especially when Zona's mother began receiving visits from her daughter's ghost complaining about her murder. City officials in Greenbrier Valley ordered an exhumation and found that the girl's neck had been broken. Her husband was immediately arrested for murder and exposed himself on the witness stand with his conflicting testimony. Mrs Heaster testified at the trial that her daughter appeared to her four nights in a row, explaining that her husband beat her in a rage for not preparing his dinner. The jury deliberated for only ten minutes before finding the husband guilty.

An even more graphic and better documented story was published by Professor James Hyslop of the American Society for Psychical Research in 1911. It concerned his investigation into the claims of Mrs Rosa Sutton, a resident of Portland, Oregon who began receiving visits from her deceased son in 1907. He had been a lieutenant at Anapolis and apparently committed suicide after a fray with some fellow officers. His apparition appeared over and over again, describing how he had been beaten and then murdered by the other officers. The apparition described in great detail where he had been wounded. Exhumation of his body confirmed that the young man was beaten in the very way the apparition claimed, though no one was ever charged with his murder.[3]

A more recent case of this nature was reported by UPI in 1970 when Mr Romer Troxell, a 42-year-old resident of Livittown, Pennsylvania, came to Portage, Indiana to take charge of his murdered son's body. It had been found by the side of a road devoid of any identification. The 'voice' of the murdered boy kept nagging at Mr Troxell's mind from the time he and his wife first arrived in town by car. He told police that the voice of his son led him to the murderer as he drove about the city looking for his son's stolen car. The voice told him right where to go, and he soon spotted the vehicle.

'I made a U-turn and followed the car, about a block behind,' he explained. 'I wanted to crash into the yellow car but Charlie warned me against it.' So he merely followed the car until the driver stopped and got out. Then he confronted the man about the car while another relative ran and fetched the police. The officers later arrested the driver on the basis of their own confidential information . . . information they had never leaked to Mr Troxell.

'Charlie left me after we caught the killer,' Troxell said. 'Charlie's in peace now. The police were on to the killer, though. I came to realize that when they later showed me what they uncovered in their investigation. But when I heard my son guiding me, I acted. Maybe the Lord wanted it that way.'[4]

Survey Evidence on the Prevalence of Subjective Contact with the Dead

Romer, Troxell, Mrs Rose Sutton, and Mrs Chua all believed that they were confronting the living presence of the dead. None of them doubted for a moment that they were experiencing anything but direct contact with the world beyond the grave. Of course it is possible that Mrs Chua's trances were psychological episodes during which her subconscious mind expressed deep-seated suspicions about Showery. It is also possible that Mr Troxell and Mrs Sutton produced their post-mortem contacts through their deep need to believe that death is not the end, perhaps reinforced by telepathically derived information. But could these episodes have actually represented genuine contacts with the dead?

This is an idea that may seem very old-fashioned and out of vogue today; but it is a theory that has to be seriously considered if for no other reason than that such reports are surprisingly common. Even though not all of these cases are as dramatic as the ones cited above, there is growing evidence that contact with the dead — or at least experiences which people believe represent such communication — is relatively frequent in our culture.

Psychologists first made this discovery in the early 1970s when they began studying the psychology of death and the mourning process. Dr W. Dewi Rees published the first major study in 1971 when he reported on 'the hallucinations of widowhood' in the *British Medical Journal*. It was an eye-opener. Rees polled 293 widows and widowers about their experiences following the deaths of their spouses and found that close to half of them (47 per cent) believed that they had been in momentary contact with them since that time. These contacts not only came immediately after the deaths, Rees learned, but sometimes even many years later. Some of the episodes were fleeting telepathic interactions, while others were fully fledged apparitional experiences. Obviously a new psychological (?) dimension to the mourning process was being uncovered. When the Rees findings were made known, researchers at Wayne State University were so intrigued that they decided to replicate the study. They obtained very similar data.

These pioneering researchers did not believe that their respondents were really communicating with the dead. They preferred to believe that they were examining some peculiar psychological aspect of the mourning process. Unfortunately, research on this idea, by Dr Richard Kalish and a colleague from the University of Southern California, in 1974, failed to demonstrate that the trauma of widowhood induces any severe psychological changes. He found no psychological difference between the widows he interviewed and a matching group of elderly women. His only significant finding was to learn once again that the bereaved reported contacts with the dead fairly commonly. But there was simply no data in his study which suggested any theory which could explain *why*.[5]

One of the problems with Dr Kalish's study was a point he couldn't have appreciated at the time. The psychologists and medical authorities pursuing the psychology of bereavement during these pioneering years worked from a questionable premise, since they believed that contact with the dead was a phenomenon restricted to the elderly or recently bereaved. What they didn't take into account was that contact with the dead is commonly reported by *all* segments of the general public. This discovery was first made later in the 1970s and has been confirmed several times sinces. The key study was once again the work of Dr Richard Kalish and David K. Reynolds, who conducted their interviews in southern California.[6] They interviewed a cross-section of the public in hopes of finding cultural differences in how people deal with death and its aftermath. The two researchers interviewed 434 adults from black, Japanese, Mexican and white (European) backgrounds and then broke their data down by race, age and sex.

The interviewers produced some amazing findings. Over 50 per cent of the women interviewed claimed spontaneous post-mortem contacts, while over a third of the men answered affirmatively as well. The experiences most often took place in dreams, but dreams described by the respondents as more vivid than usual. Visits from the dead by way of voices, apparitions, or psychologically felt presences were also mentioned.

This last feature was a little out of keeping with the experience of widowhood, where the 'felt presence' is rather commonly reported. The psychologists also noted that the experiences they heard about were pleasant more often than frightening, and that on rare occasions other people who were present shared the experiences.

This was an amazing admission, though it was a feature that the psychologists ultimately ignored when they came to interpreting their findings. They were obviously more interested in the demographics of what they were finding. Culture obviously didn't influence the expression of the experience, since Kalish and Reynolds found that all ethnic groups reported similar types of cases. Their most significant findings were that blacks and Mexican-Americans reported the experience more often than Caucasians or Orientals. The two former groups also found the experience more frightening and reported more visual and auditory contacts. (These two features may not have been mutually independent, since one finding may easily have arisen from the other.)

Despite its pioneering nature, the Kalish/Reynolds study was — in the long run — somewhat flawed in its conclusions. Reporting bias may have played a significant role in the overall statistics, a problem the psychologists did little to explore or even acknowledge. They concluded that culture definitely affected the subjective experience of contacting the dead, without considering whether certain groups in American culture merely *report* such contacts more readily. It might also be that people from different ethnic and social backgrounds are more willing to talk about such experiences or, on the other hand, more prone to rationalize them away. The two psychologists should have been aware of this possibility, since the actual *mode* of the experience (i.e. what form it took) did not vary with any demographic factors. Obviously they were dealing with a cross-cultural phenomenon.

The two Californian researchers couldn't even find any correlation between the strength of the witnesses' religious beliefs and the likelihood of their reporting post-mortem contacts. In fact, those respondents who did not consider themselves especially religious actually reported spontaneous contacts with the dead more often than did the devoutly religious. The less educated tended to report the experience more often than other respondents, but this finding probably resulted from an important confounding variable I will describe later. The researchers also discovered, to their amazement, that '. . . widows and other people who have lost intimate relationships [did] not account for as large a proportion of the experiences as we had anticipated.' The only exception was the black sub-group.

In short, no purely psychological basis for these experiences could be found. This did not keep Dr Kalish from personally dismissing the metaphysical reality of post-mortem contact experiences, however. His final conclusion was that, 'I do not believe that these people have engaged in communication with the dead.' He added that 'I do believe that the experiences were both very vivid and seem very real, that they are neither dreams nor indications of emotional disturbance.' So just what does he think these encounters do represent?

'They are signals,' he has explained, 'that the intensity of the loss or other experience is extremely great and extremely enduring; and that the previously formed associations with the dead person were extremely strong.' His conclusion is that the alleged contact springs from the witnesses' own minds.

Despite his personal conclusions, Dr Kalish's pioneering work has helped to illuminate this aspect of the psychology of death. It is clear that 'contact with the dead' is a very common feeling and that such experiences occur in divergent cultures, are expressed very similarly, and are experienced by people of all age groups. This counters the idea that such experiences primarily result from bereavement. Yet the Kalish/Reynolds data are not unique. Very similar features cropped up when a team of researchers in Chicago replicated the Kalish/Reynolds work.[7] They found that 25 per cent of their subject population of close to 1500 respondents reported spontaneous contacts with the dead. The elderly and teenagers were especially prone to report the experience. The researchers also found (like their predecessors) that blacks were particularly prone to claim post-mortem contacts, and that Jews and Protestants reported the experience more often than Catholics. Unlike their colleagues in California, however, the Chicago researchers were well aware that many of their findings might merely represent artefacts. The experiences of widows and widowers did not bias the data, though once again it looked as if the less educated more freely experienced or discussed the experience than the better educated. The researchers were able to show definitively that this finding was spurious. It resulted because elderly people in our culture, who are most prone to report such experiences, are typically less educated than younger Americans.

Spontaneous Post-Mortem Contacts

If there were any glaring problems with these surveys, they were experiential rather than statistical ones. Neither those researchers working from California nor those from Illinois really seemed to be very interested in the *content* of what their respondents were reporting. They never concerned themselves with the human dimensions of what they were learning. Were these people really in contact with the dead or not? The answer to this crucial question cannot be answered through statistics, but only through case studies.

This problem was partially corrected in 1980 when Julian Burton decided to study the same issue but from a more humanistic framework. Burton was working on his Ph.D in psychology when he decided to use his data as the basis for his doctoral dissertation. Dr Burton has explained that the idea for his project grew out of a dramatic personal experience. His mother died in April 1973 at the age of 67 after suffering a massive stroke. 'I had always felt a strong bond between us,' he later wrote, 'but by September most of us in the family had returned to our normal routines, reconciled to her death.'

But this was not to be the end of the bond between Dr Burton and his mother. 'One evening that September my wife and I were entertaining relatives,' he explains. 'I was in the kitchen cutting a pineapple when I heard what I thought were my wife's footsteps behind me to the right. I turned to ask the whereabouts of a bowl but realized that she had crossed to the left outside my field of vision. I turned in that direction to repeat my question *and saw my mother standing there*. She was fully visible, looking years younger than at the time of her death. She was wearing a diaphanous pale-blue gown trimmed in marabou which I had never seen before...'

No sooner could he call out than the figure gradually dissolved. 'The next morning I called my sister Jean and told her what had happened', the psychologist continued. 'She was upset and began to sob, asking why our mother had not come to *her*. I felt bad about this and asked her if she believed that I had told her, whereupon she said she *knew* it was true. Why was she so certain? She replied that she and Mother had gone shopping together two weeks before the stroke and Mother had tried on the pale-blue gown I had described. Although Mother looked attractive in the dress and wanted it very much, she had balked at paying $200 for such a garment.'[8]

The result of this visit was that at the age of 42, Burton decided to go back and finish his doctorate. 'My mother's appearance gave me the idea for my research', he admits. 'I felt that many people probably have similar experiences to tell.'

Burton thereupon devised a questionnaire which asked the respondents whether they had ever experienced visitations from the dead, their relationship to the revenants, the nature of the experiences, whether they were repeated, and so forth. He first gave the questionnaire to psychic research groups and classes in the Los Angeles area, but he soon changed his strategy when he noticed the extraordinarily high percentage of affirmative answers. His suspicion was that his respondents were biased by their interest in psychic matters, so he sent out questionnaires to the psychology departments of three Los Angeles colleges. Fifty per cent of the students *still* reported post-mortem contacts! Dr Burton has, to date, collected data from 1500 respondents and has added important data to the earlier polls from California and Illinois. He, too, found that the elderly are especially prone to such contacts though they have no monopoly on them. The majority of experiences were either dream contacts or subjective sensations, although voices, waking visions, and apparitions were also reported. These experiences were obviously dramatic since 60 per cent of those between the ages of 16 and 60 changed their attitudes about death on the basis of them.[9]

What really impressed Burton, though, were the cases themselves. Some of them were so similar to his own. 'Nearing the completion of my dissertation', he later wrote,

> . . . I was working at home while my occasional housekeeper Lita Canales, a woman in her 30s, was cleaning. She came to me and told me two stories, one of which happened while she was in my home.
>
> While cleaning my bedroom one day Lita heard a 'wolf whistle'. Thinking a workman outside the window was looking in (although I live on the third floor) she continued her work. The whistle sounded again. When she looked

up she heard a woman's voice call her twice by name. She looked through the other rooms and found no one. Despite a cold chill and goose bumps she thought no more of it until she arrived home to find a letter from El Salvador with the news of the death of her best friend. Her friend's mother wrote that Lita's gift of a pair of new shoes arrived three hours before the death. This news triggered Lita's memory; the wolf whistle had been a girlhood signal between her friend and her. The clarity and simplicity of this report are typical of many that I have heard and read in the course of my research.

Another case was reported to Burton by a young college student and concerned the death of his great-aunt. They obviously didn't share the type of bond that might give rise to a strong emotional attachment, thereby inducing an apparently anomalous psychological experience:

> I heard of her death as soon as I got home from school. I had to hurry off, however, to go to my catechism class. I went up to my room to get my book and as I was reaching for it, I stopped and slowly turned around. Sitting on my other bed was a slightly transparent woman with her hands folded in her lap. She just sat there smiling at me. I had not seen her since I was six months old but somehow I knew it was my great-aunt who had just died. We had corresponded for years through letters and I still correspond with her sister, with whom she lived. I realized what was happening but I wasn't frightened because I was almost overwhelmed with this intense feeling of love. There was nothing threatening or disturbing about the experience at all. I stood very still and purposefully started memorizing details of what she looked like, what dress she was wearing and so on. When she was gone I went downstairs and told my mother and sister what had happened. If I was ever afraid of death, I'm not anymore. I strongly believe in some sort of life after death. I'm not sure that if another family member had had an experience, they would have said so.

What is also significant is how Dr Burton came to view his data. He feels that experiences such as his own and those he has collected tend to go unreported all too often. He argues that many people are simply afraid that their sanity will be questioned if they report such encounters. This problem has been exacerbated, claims the psychologist, by mental health professionals who try to 'explain away' such episodes. These experiences are usually dismissed as attempts by the witness to 'hold on' to the dead or as hallucinations deriving from the grieving process. 'But do we have the right to do this?' he asks. 'I hope others will investigate this phenomenon,' he urges, 'and add their information to the growing pile of evidence that these experiences are normal and common. Perhaps eventually the sensational and scary nature of "campfire"-type ghost stories will give way to the realization that experiencing visits from the dead may be a commonplace function of day-to-day living.'

Despite the very emotional and often impressive nature of these human experiences, the sceptic could still have a field-day dismissing them. Few such cases ever turn out to be as veridical as Dr Burton's, and even fewer are of the quality that would have impressed the founders of psychical research a hundred years ago. Most of the reports can easily be dismissed, as Dr Burton suggests, as simply the wish-fulfilment fantasies of generally unhappy and bereaved people. Even the more complex cases in which some psychic factor played an obvious role can often be reduced to more 'this worldly' explanations. For instance, perhaps Dr Burton used some homespun clairvoyance while unconsciously generating the apparition of his mother, and so forth. Survival research often becomes bogged down in such issues, the same issues that so confounded the first psychical researchers back in Victorian times.

Dream Contact with the Dead

It is significant that most researchers interested in spontaneous contacts with the dead have found dream contacts to be the most common mode of expression. Yet this is the easiest form of post-mortem contact to dismiss. This fact, however, has not led researchers to abandon this line of inquiry completely. The late Dr Robert Crookall, a British scientist who sacrificed his pension in order to throw himself into survival research, long argued that some dream contacts may be instigated by surviving intelligences. He argued the point in his book 'Dreams' of High Significance, which appeared in 1974. Mrs Helen Solem of Portland, Oregon has recently reopened this question by undertaking a large collection of such cases. She currently divides her time between her accounting work and survival research, and undertook her dream project in 1983 as a result of her own dream experiences. Soon she began collecting the reports of others and was able to amass a sizeable body of material. My own interest in Mrs Solem's project arose from my concern with the publication of veridical cases of post-mortem contact. So when I first learned that the Portland researcher was initiating her project, I requested that she be on the look out for cases which included the communication of evidential material. Several of these cases were later submitted to Fate magazine (on whose staff I serve as consulting editor).[10]

Some of the accounts Mrs Solem collected were relatively simple. One elderly lady told the researcher that she had a dream in 1906 in which she heard her deceased brother talking to her. The voice informed her that she had to make an important choice — one between her latest born child (then a year and a half old) and the one she was carrying.

The voice was firm on the matter, and the woman reluctantly chose to keep the baby that was about to be born. The upshot of the dream came about three weeks later, when the older girl fell from the porch, injured her head, and died. 'When reporting this experience now,' explains Mrs Solem, 'she says she believes it was given to her to help her through that calamitous time.' The warning helped her to retain her sanity and keep her grief from overwhelming her. The sceptic will of course scoff that perhaps — granting that this experience was genuinely psychic — the woman's own mind generated the prediction. This would be a reasonable assumption to make, except that not all of Mrs Solem's cases are that easy to deal with.

In another of her cases, a woman from Connecticut explained how her deceased father-in-law came to her in her sleep the day after his funeral. His purpose was to inform her about a secret bank book hidden in his room which held the key to $2800. Even her husband derided the story until a search disclosed the bankbook. The holdings in the account matched the sum communicated in the dream.

Another one of these rather complex cases was reported by a housewife Solem merely called by her first name, Gwen. 'Until my mother passed away in 1959,' she explained, 'I don't specifically remember if I ever dreamed of anyone deceased or not. However, I was very distraught over my mother's death at the early age of 49. Many times after that she came to me in my dreams, especially when I was perplexed or disturbed about something.' The woman soon learned that she could ask her mother's advice and that the dream-figure would readily answer.

One night, for instance, she dreamed about a room full of coffins and intuitively realized that her father was going to die. She became alarmed but her mother appeared and comforted her, promising to help her former husband through the death experience. The sequel to the drama came a few days later when her brother called from Virginia to inform her that their father was in hospital. His condition was bad, he was haemorrhaging and the doctors wanted to perform vein bypass surgery. Gwen knew that the surgery would be fruitless, but she wanted her father to have every chance he could. It came as no surprise when the man died four days later . . . but Gwen didn't initially learn about the death through normal hospital or family channels. Early that morning her mother came to her in a dream and told her that everything was 'all over' now. Gwen woke up and saw that it was 7 o'clock. The hospital phoned only later to say that her father had died at 7.10 that morning. When she retired the night after the funeral a few days later, she asked if she might see her father in her dream and talk with him. Her mother came to her once again and explained that such a meeting could only come later, after the elderly man adjusted himself to his new spiritual existence. This dream contact came in due course six months later.

It is Mrs Solem's opinion that something more than simple dreaming is being manifested in such cases. 'Some authorities believe that dream activity is simply a way of restoring emotional balance by ridding ourselves of the stress and tension of the day,' she argues. 'But when some clear, straightforward and heretofore unknown information comes through our dreams, it must be more than this . . . It is possible such dreams come through the help of our own higher selves, but when the dead appear in our dreams it seems logical to conclude that a mutual working relationship is manifesting.'

This is, of course, the fatal catch. Is it ever possible to determine where the activity of one's mind ends and that of an external intelligence begins? This is the problem the researcher faces when trying to evaluate subjective human experiences, always so complex and subtle.

Other Forms of Post-Mortem Contact

Some researchers have begun studying the literature on death-bed visions to help resolve this issue. Such cases represent an important addition to the literature on survival evidence, but they can only be briefly discussed here.

Patients on the verge of death often 'see' apparitions of the dead coming to greet them and take them to the 'other side'. The early psychical researchers even collected a few cases in which the dying person saw a friend *whom he did not know had only recently died.* But these cases are rare. The real breakthrough came in the 1960s and 1970s when Dr Karlis Osis at the American Society for Psychical Research was able to show that many of these dying patients were not suffering from any disease or responding to any medication known to prompt the emergence of hallucinations. Later he and his colleague, Dr Erlendur Haraldsson of the University of Reykjavik in Iceland, were able to show that deathbed visions were a cross-cultural phenomenon.[11] The significant point is that, once again, psychological inquiry has shown that subjective contact with the dead (be it through visions, dreams, or felt presences) simply can't be explained by any known normal mechanism.

Even Dr Osis would admit that such cases cannot serve as indisputable evidence for life after death, though. Some undefined psychological factors may be underlying their emergence. So he has personally gone back to the study of apparitions in general, in hopes of finding some evidence for survival. The one case to which he points most proudly was a complex one that he first reported to the 26th annual convention of the Parapsychological Association at Fairleigh Dickinson University in 1983.[12]

Dr Osis began his presentation by entertaining the possibility that not all apparitions represent the outcome of a single psychic process. 'I have stressed on other occasions', he reminded his audience, 'that apparitional experiences make much more sense when we allow ourselves to postulate special interpretations of each of the different kinds of apparitional experiences, rather than to lump them all together as if they were of the same fundamental nature.' He added that 'this present case is a specimen of one type of apparition experience [in which] the appearer seems to have a purpose of his own.' These were brave words about a phenomenon currently out of vogue among parapsychologists exploring the survival controversy.

Since the parties involved in the report insisted on absolute anonymity, Dr Osis had to disguise their identities. The case revolved around the death of a middle-aged married businessman named Leslie, who was the father of four children. The other *persona dramatis* in the story was the gentleman's deceased son, Rusty, who had died as a young child eighteen months before. Leslie's death occurred in 1982 when the private plane he was piloting across the southern part of the United States crashed. What actually caused the accident is still unknown, and the family was informed of the accident the next day. Their main concern, apart from their own grief, was with Leslie's ageing mother, Marge, who was experiencing health problems of her own. They were afraid that the news of the death would be too great a shock for her to handle. A friend of the family shared this concern. Being devoutly religious, she asked her own mother — who was the same age as Leslie's mother — to pray for the departed soul. This woman knew that Leslie's mother was rather materialistic and harboured no belief in anything psychic or spiritual. So she prayed directly to the deceased man and asked him to appear to his mother as a 'sign' of his continued existence. She also asked in her prayer that, as a personal sign to her, he should appear holding hands with his recently deceased son. The woman told no one except her husband about her prayer, and she repeated the petition about three times over the next couple of days.

Marge was home in her room about ten hours after these prayers were being concluded. She awoke from sleep suddenly to see two apparitional forms at the foot of her bed.

'There he was, Leslie, with the baby', she later told Dr Osis, 'and he was holding the baby's hand . . . they were at the foot of the bed. They looked at each other. I was wide awake then. They were content; they were happy that they found each other, that they were together now. And they were letting me know that it is so. I got that feeling.'

She also explained to Dr Osis:

They were solid. There was like grayness around, like a gray cloud around them. I would say there was a mist in the whole room, nothing you could touch, just the grayness all around. But they were solid, both of them. The room was dark; electric light was coming from outside through the venetian blinds . . . but I didn't need light to see them. There is a lot of traffic around my area. No matter at what time you got trucks and buses. Not one sound then, all was excluded at that moment, everything, as though the world had stood still. And there was nobody but us three in the world . . .

I felt them as if they were breathing into me, breathing my life into me. He was giving my life back to me. And it's the most lasting feeling: I will never, never forget this. Never, never forget this. It never happened before and never happened since. They were just there, I believe, to give me peace of mind. It really helped. I have not gotten over [the grief] yet, but it made me able to live through very hard times without killing myself, because I was very despondent. I tried to keep them longer and they just went . . . They got smaller and faded out.

But Marge wasn't the only person who experienced a phantasmal visitation that night. Leslie's little six-year-old niece lived about a hundred miles away. She knew about her uncle's death and saw his apparition three hours *before* the visitation to Marge. She later told Dr Osis that she was 'up and awake when I saw a cloud in my room and there was Leslie and Rusty holding hands. They looked just regular . . . it looked just like him [Leslie]! It is interesting that the woman who prayed to Leslie could hardly have been thinking of the girl; she didn't even know that he had any nieces.

Dr Osis feels that the super-ESP hypothesis would have to be extended completely out of proportion to account for this case, since Marge didn't really respond to the purported telepathic message until several hours after it had (allegedly) been sent. He also found it odd that the little niece would have responded to such a message, since she didn't know the woman who prayed. Nor does it look as though she picked up the information from the older woman, since the little girl's experience came three hours before Marge's. They weren't even very close.

The presentation of this case to the Parapsychological Association ended with both a conclusion and a warning. 'One case alone cannot decide the survival issue,' advised Dr Osis. 'Different scholars will interpret the data differently, each according to their own belief systems. The manifest characteristics of this case certainly do not suggest the notion that apparitions are static images void of consciousness. Something much more powerful and purposeful seems to be indicated.'

So as parapsychology enters into its second century of enquiry, those researchers studying the survival question have apparently come full circle. From the study of real-life encounters with the unknown, they have searched through the realms of trance mediumship, out-of-body experiences, deathbed visions, and near-death encounters to demonstrate man's immortality. It now seems as though parapsychologists have found themselves once again focusing on the apparitional experience as their most potentially fruitful source of study.

5.

Tape-Recorded 'Spirit' Voices: Delusion or Breakthrough?

Ever since parapsychology first became a science, students of the field have wondered whether some sort of instrumental or electronic communications channel could be established between the living and the dead. Both Thomas Edison and Guglielmo Marconi firmly maintained that a machine could be built capable of linking together the material and the psychic worlds. They even outlined rough designs for such devices. A 'psychic telephone' was actually built in the 1920s, but made little lasting impression on psychical researchers. Like its inventor, it soon just faded from sight — and sound — shortly after its invention. Meanwhile, an eccentric Dutchman turned up in England in the 1940s with blueprints for a 'spirit radio', but nothing ever came of that either.

Although no one has yet come up with a sure-fire psychic telephone, ever since the 1920s there have been instances where the 'voices of the dead' have been spontaneously heard to speak over radios, record player amplifiers, and more recently, electromagnetic tape. And this latter phenomenon — that the voices of the dead can be caught and imprinted on tape — has been one of the most controversial topics in contemporary parapsychology. It is a debate that is still going on, and it's just as heated as ever.

This phenomenon first achieved worldwide attention in 1959 when Freidrich Jurgenson, a 60-year-old former opera singer and film-maker, claimed that he had successfully tape-recorded the voice of his deceased mother, and further maintained that *anyone* using the proper procedures could pick up the voices of the dead on their own tape recorders. Just how Jurgenson made his discovery is a matter of controversy, though, since the experimenter has given two different versions of the story. Back in the 1960s Jurgenson claimed that he accidentally discovered the taped-voice phenomenon while taping bird-songs in his backyard. On replaying the tape, he asserted, he found the voice of his mother calling out his name imprinted between the bird-songs. Jurgenson was, of course, so surprised by the incident that he tried to replicate it by systematically recording bird-songs or by merely leaving his tape recorder running while engaging in normal conversation with his living friends and relatives. Often, he stoutly maintained, he would find extra voices on the tapes when they were replayed. Sometimes they would call out the names of the people present in the room, and occasionally even comment on the previous conversation!

Jurgenson changed this story around a bit in 1973, however, during an interview he gave to *Psychic News,* a London spiritualist weekly, in which he gave what is presumably a more complete account of his discovery.

'I find it extremely difficult to describe exactly why I carried out these experiments,' he told the reporters. 'Somehow, and completely without any known reason there grew in me an overwhelming desire to establish electronic contact with something or somebody unknown. It was a strange feeling; almost as if I had to open a channel for something which was still hidden and wanted to get into the open. At the same time I remember feeling sceptical, amused and curious.'

This intuitive 'overwhelming desire' occurred in the autumn of 1958, but it wasn't until July 1959 that the hunch paid off. As he told *Psychic News:*

> After a somewhat unnerving experience during a recording of the song of the Swedish finch, when I first assumed that my tape-recorder had suffered damage during the journey from the city into the country, I realized that the mix-up on the tape-recording could not be explained away as a coincidence. A few weeks later I went to a small forest hut and attempted another experiment. I did, of course, have no idea what I was looking for. I put the microphone in the window. The recording I made passed without incident. On playback I first heard some twittering of birds in the distance, then silence. Suddenly, from nowhere a voice, a woman's voice in German: 'Friedel, my little Friedel, can you hear me?'
>
> It was as if the speaker had to make a tremendous effort to speak and the voice sounded anxious. But I am sure beyond a shadow of doubt that this was the unmistakable voice of my mother who called me by name. My mother had died four years earlier in Sweden. That was how it began.

Jurgenson's claim, no matter how trail-blazing or bizarre, made little impact on international parapsychology. Although his 'discovery' made headlines in the press, practically no serious students of parapsychology paid much attention to his claims. Since most parapsychologists during the '60s were much more interested in playing with ESP cards or trying to influence rolling dice than studying psychic contact with the dead, the psychic community merely snored through Jurgenson's breakthrough. Only one parapsychlogist even bothered to test Jurgenson personally. W. G. Roll, project director for the Psychical Research Foundation, based in Durham, North Carolina paid a week-long visit to Jurgenson at his home outside of Stockholm in 1964.[1] Jurgenson was more than willing to give his visitor a test series of demonstrations, and Roll later issued a report, 'Spirit Voices of Freidrich Jurgensen'[sic] on behalf of the P.R.F. Judging by the report, Roll's tests were moderately successful.

For each session, Jurgenson merely took a blank tape, placed it on his machine, and then left the machine running and the microphone open as everyone in the room engaged in a little relaxed conversation. The tape was stopped at frequent intervals and replayed.

'On four occasions there were slight indistinct sounds which could, however, quite easily have been produced by those present,' writes Roll. Then,

> . . . a male voice seemed to say the Swedish word 'beratta' ('tell or relate') during a pause in the conversation. None of us remembered having said or heard the word during the preceding discussion. It was quite distinct.
> We then did an additional four . . . tests . . . F. J. said in his normal voice on the tape 'We can wait a little,' three small taps were heard, followed by the word 'warten' (German, 'wait') which was heard quite clearly . . . finally, six tappings, spaced in three pairs, were heard quite clearly and seemed to say 'ta' de' retta kontakt' (Swedish, 'take the right contact') but the words were not clear . . .'

Since first discovering the taped-voice effect, Jurgenson has made several new claims and has developed new methods for taping the voices. The Swedish experimenter now often tapes directly from a radio. He hooks his recording equipment to a radio which has been pre-set on an interband white noise frequency, tapes for several minutes, and then replays the result. Sometimes, claims Jurgenson, quite clear voices will be heard speaking *through* the background white noise. He also claims that occasionally human voices speaking over the radio on a commercial wavelength, when recorded, will be skilfully distorted and rearranged by the 'voice-entities' so as to deliver new words and messages. The voices presumably speak in a mixture of languages on occasion.

The History of Taped-Voice-Research

Actually, though, Jurgenson in no way really 'discovered' the taped-voice phenomenon. While he was carrying out his experiments in Sweden, similar investigations had already been underway for two years in the United States and were about to be published by Raymond Bayless, a parapsychologist, and Attila von Szalay, a psychic, who accidentally discovered the taped-voice effect in 1956.[2] They carried out their joint research until the 1960s, and then resumed their work in the 1970s by which time I had joined them. Art (as we will call von Szalay) is now in his early seventies and has somewhat retired from his investigations, but the Bayless and von Szalay work undoubtedly constitutes *the* most important chapter in the history of the taped-voice research.

Bayless first got the idea for their joint effort when Art, whom he had met through mutual friends, told him that he sometimes heard 'independent voices' (voices produced out of thin air) speaking to him when he was alone. He had first noticed the voices in 1938, he told Bayless, when he heard the voice of his deceased son call out his name. In 1941 he tried recording the voices on an old 78 r.p.m. record cutter, but without success. Raymond was so tantalized by Art's claim that he decided to pursue this line of investigation further, hoping to eventually tape record these 'psychic voices'. He had no way of knowing at the time that he would accidentally help discover the taped-voice effect.

Raymond initiated his first three-year project by renting a Hollywood studio (still there even today above Hollywood's famous Pickwick Bookstore at the intersection of Hollywood Blvd and McCadden Place) where he constructed a small wooden enclosure or 'cabinet' which roughly resembled a clothes-closet. Inside they placed a microphone resting in the mouth of a speaking trumpet, while a cable was run from the mike to a loudspeaker and tape machine *outside* the enclosure. That way, the experimenters could hear any sounds or voices produced inside the cabinet while sitting anywhere in the studio. All the experiments, of course, were taped.

For their first tests, Art would sit inside the cabinet and within moments Raymond was able to hear whispering voices coming over the loudspeaker. In order to assure himself that Art wasn't producing the voices himself, Raymond conducted several additional tests during which Art sat *outside* the cabinet. Sure enough, voices and whispers came through the loudspeaker even when the wooden enclosure was absolutely empty! Von Szalay and Bayless used this procedure to make several tapes of the voices. It wasn't until several weeks later, though, that they discovered that sometimes voices would appear on the tapes which they had *not* heard over the loudspeaker. This crucial discovery was made on 5 December 1956. As Raymond states in a report on the von Szalay voices, published in the *Journal* of the American Society for Psychical Research:

Mr von Szalay, for the purpose of this particular experiment, sat in the cabinet alone for fifteen minutes. Believing that nothing was forthcoming, he left the cabinet. We then played back the tape recording expecting to hear nothing, but were surprised to hear a distinct voice say, 'This is G.' At this time I was sitting on the outside of the cabinet listening to the highly amplified loud speaker and heard absolutely nothing.

I then decided to make certain tests of the amplifying system and we both stood a few feet from the closed cabinet door and each other in full sight while Mr von Szalay made single whistles at short intervals. I was listening to the loud speaker when I suddenly realized that we were receiving low whistles in answer. I then told Mr von Szalay when to whistle and each time answering whistles were heard. There were at least six or seven answering whistles and at the end of this sequence, double whistles replied. We were standing within three feet of each other and were able to observe each other closely. The room was normally illuminated and fraud, under such conditions, is completely eliminated.

The 5 December experiment conclusively demonstrated that von Szalay was able not only to produce disembodied voices, but somehow to get them to appear directly on tape as well. Consequently, Raymond decided to carry out a more stringent experiment to prove the existence of von Szalay's voices. For the pilot test he procured a large upright cardboard box in which he placed the microphone and trumpet which in turn led to a recording machine several feet away. The experimenters then sat a yard away from the box, turned on the tape, and replayed it at intervals. Three distinct voices were heard on the tape, but were garbled to such an extent that they couldn't be deciphered. (I've encountered this type of reception with von Szalay very often. The psychic voices will be almost as loud as our own, but so 'mush-mouthed' that they cannot be understood. Anyone who had had some experience with a bad quality tape-recorder phone-answering system will recognize the similarity.)

Raymond carried out a follow-up experiment which was run under even more stringent conditions. He covered the box containing the microphone with a heavy camel-pile overcoat and the entire set-up was then placed in another large box. Both boxes were suspended from the ceiling of the cabinet, while von Szalay and Raymond sat several feet away outside the enclosure. A cable led from the microphone to the tape machine which was also placed outside the cabinet. The results were just as successful, and they were able to record human whispers on the tape.

Later that same night, after Raymond had left, Art decided to continue with the experiments himself by sitting in the cabinet with the tape running and replaying it at intervals. Since he had not heard any independent voices while sitting in the cabinet, he naturally thought that his test had been a complete failure. But on replaying the tape, he discovered that he had successfully recorded a female voice saying, 'Hot dog, Art!' quite loudly. The voice even twittered off with a high-pitched laugh. Von Szalay realized that while this clear voice had been impressed on the tape, it had bypassed his own ear. The voice also had a special meaning for him. Years before he had dated a young woman in New York during the improverished depression years. They were sweethearts of sorts, but could only afford to dine at the local hot dog stand where they could buy two hot dogs for a nickle. They often joked about their dinners, promising each other they would always remember them. Art had not seen or heard from his old flame in years and she was presumably dead.

Despite the fact that they publicly reported on their work in 1959, Bayless and von Szalay, like Jurgenson, failed to catch the interest of the parapsychological community at large. Neither of them received so much as one letter of inquiry about their experiments after the *Journal* of the American Society for Psychical Research published their findings.

The Work of Konstantine Raudive

Today, though, the picture has somewhat changed. In 1970 a Latvian scholar living in Germany, Dr Konstantine Raudive, shocked the English-speaking parapsychological community with his book, *Breakthrough*, which had been previously published in Germany. Raudive had worked with Jurgenson personally and claimed that he himself had been able to obtain these mysterious voices on tape . . . and was willing to demonstrate the fact for anyone inclined to listen.[3] Raudive made several other claims about his own taped-voice effects, many of which closely matched some of Jurgenson's original findings. He maintained, for example, that the voices often speak in a polyglot mixture of languages; that they will answer direct questions if any are addressed to them during the taping sessions; and that anybody — psychic or not — can record these voices if they experiment long and diligently enough. However, Raudive disdained the 'open mike' technique so often employed by Jurgenson (though he did use it on occasion), and preferred to hook his tape directly to a radio set on a white noise band. This was, once again, a recording technique he borrowed from Jurgenson. This method did present some problems though. Since his voices were usually weak, sceptics merely assumed that Raudive was picking up fragments of commercial broadcasts. And it didn't help much when he did accidentally tape-record a Radio Luxemburg broadcast!

This theory, though often spouted by his critics, really doesn't explain

Konstantine Raudive, the Latvian psychologist who helped to establish the
Electronic Voice Phenomenon as evidence that the dead were communicating
via recording devices. (Mary Evans Picture Library)

the wide gamut of Raudive's taped-voice effects, however. While it is true that he did occasionally pick up radio signals which were often misinterpreted as taped voices, on many occasions his 'voices' would call out his name quite clearly. Even many of his critics had to admit that. For example, Trinity College in Cambridge, England, issued its 1970 studentship in psychical research to David Ellis, a young chemist, to investigate the Raudive voices. Although Ellis never came to any decision about the paranormality of the taped-voice phenomenon, he did admit in the February, 1974 issue of *Psychic* magazine that:

> With Dr Raudive present, the voices sometimes refer directly to the other participants, but at other times they speak mainly to Dr Raudive (nicknamed 'Kosti'). There are some interesting comments when he is absent. The recording may start with 'We need Kosti' or 'We need Kosti here', or a voice may explain, 'You have hidden Kosti.'[4]

Before his recent death, Raudive allowed himself to be scientifically tested on many occasions and participated in a number of 'test' demonstrations throughout Europe. When the British publishing firm of Colin Smythe Ltd was considering issuing a British edition of his book, Raudive even travelled to Great Britain in order to personally demonstrate for his prospective publishers just how he conducted his experiments. The results of his trip were interesting, to say the least, and a controlled experiment was set up on 13 December 1969 by Colin Smythe and Peter Bander at a London recording studio. Their idea was to have a recording engineer, trained in the art and problems of delicate recording techniques, supervise the experiment. David Stanley, a qualified radio engineer, was chosen and the experiments were conducted in his studio. Raudive at first seemed to have trouble picking up the 'voices' in this strange new environment and several brief taping sessions were complete failures. But this was not the end of the matter: 'During the next half an hour', Bander reminisces in his preface to *Breakthrough*,

> . . . a number of my guests talked to Dr Raudive on technical points, and one of them indicated that the only proof he was now willing to accept would be something definite; for example, if a voice were to give the name of a person present. As it was highly unlikely that such a name would be 'floating in the air' from some radio station, it would prove to him that a voice was trying to make a deliberate contact.
> Meantime Mr Stanley had disconnected the additional four inches of wire from the diode and connected the original diode to the radio input, letting the tape run. I think the tape had only been running about two minutes (by now we had used the fourth tape because each time an experiment

had been made, we opened a new tape), when Dr Raudive asked Stanley to play the recording back. With about twenty people talking and wishing each other a Merry Christmas, it was most surprising when four of them suddenly rushed to the tape-recorder. There, clear and without a shadow of doubt, a rhythmic voice, twice the speed of human voice said, *'Raudive there'* — Mr Stanley was perhaps the most surprised of them all, because according to his explanation there just could not be any voice on the tape. But there was a voice and it called the name of the one person who was most concerned with it all.

If anything, the ability to get taped-voice effects on electromagnetic tape is contagious. Since publishing *Breakthrough,* both Bander and Smythe have been taping these articulations themselves.

Taped-Voice Research Today

The early experiments of Raudive, Jurgenson and von Szalay are now psychic history. Nevertheless, many people still entertain some major misconceptions about the tape-voice phenomenon. For example, these voices are not, as some critics maintain, merely fleeting and almost random articulations. Sometimes they will impart lengthy and clear messages or answer specific questions. Von Szalay's voices have an absolute penchant for making directly pertinent comments to either Art or to those taking part in a taping session with him. Two examples of this phenomenon, drawn from the records of two different researchers, aptly prove this fact.

On 20 September 1971, Raymond Bayless and his wife were having a snack together in the kitchen of their West Los Angeles home. Raymond was in a rather bad humour that day and told Marjorie that he would like to divorce himself from the rest of the world. Marjorie replied by telling her husband about a friend who actually had cut himself off from the rest of humanity and had become a *recluse.* (This word was actually used during the course of the conversation.) Raymond's reaction to the story was predictable . . . he expressed envy for the man.

Unknown to the Baylesses, Art was experimenting with his tape recorder at his own apartment some fifteen miles away in Van Nuys, California. At the very time Raymond and Marjorie were having their discussion, Art taped a voice saying, 'Bayless has virtually become a recluse.'

An even more bizarre taped voice actually made headlines in Europe! Dr Franz Seidl, an Austrian engineer who was one of Raudive's original co-workers, is still actively engaged in taped-voice research and can himself pick up psychic voices on his own tapes. As a result of his work with Raudive, though, Seidl in the late 1960s began to theorize that there must be a more efficient way to procure the voices on tape than by the 'open mike' or radio techniques his mentor was using. Being an electrical engineer by profession, he eventually invented a handy little gadget called a *psychophone* — a miniature wide frequency radio receiver coupled with an amplifier. (Any voices produced over the instrument will thus be automatically amplified while simultaneously recorded). Seidl's work hit the presses when he announced that his 'voices' had given him information about a kidnapping case that had stymied the police.[5]

Seidl first got the idea for his bizarre experiment in the summer of 1970 when the press began carrying stories about the disappearance of a young woman who had vanished while on a camping trip. Seidl decided to ask the 'voices' about the missing girl and received the reply 'Emmanua, in mare con dimetiatis Paolo' over the psychophone during a subsequent taping session. The girl's parents heard about the test, got in touch with Seidl, and publicly admitted that one of the campers who had accompanied their daughter was a young Italian named Paolo.

The case was unfortunately never solved, so we will never know just how pertinent Seidl's message really was. But the case is yet another proof that these taped 'voices' — whatever their nature — are able to answer questions and make meaningful replies or comments when called upon to do so. These incidents also help us to understand a little about the nature of the voices. Any voices that can call out the names of the experimenters or answer specific questions are not merely radio pick-ups!

Unfortunately, there is no denying that most tape-recorded 'spirit' voices are vague, capricious, and sometimes hard to decipher. This is undoubtedly the reason that this area of research has never caught on within conventional parapsychology. Another problem with this line of research is that the quality of the results does not seem to be dependent on the equipment used. The usual meagre number of voices and low amplitude of their speech seems the same no matter whether a Soni portable or a $5000 reel-to-reel set-up is used and this, too, has discouraged would-be researchers.

The fact that most tape-recorded 'spirit voices' are admittedly fleeting and markedly unloquacious has led many researchers to wonder if one day a breakthrough might come that will make this form of contact with the dead more facile and extended. And this leads directly to what is undoubtedly the most recent and 'hottest' development in the area of tape-recorded voice research . . . i.e. the publicity over Mr George Meek and his Spiricom machine.

Towards the end of 1982 George Meek, a retired businessman living in North Carolina, announced that he had been involved in a related line of research since 1971.[6] That was the year he opened a private laboratory in Philadelphia in collaboration with Mr William J. O'Neill, an amateur electronics engineer who has spent years developing a complex machine through which the voices of the dead can allegedly manifest. O'Neill eventually claimed that he had made contact with Dr George Mueller, an American physicist who died in 1967 and who gave enough information that his life was successfully traced. Regular communications via this machine (which was soon dubbed Spiricom) were first achieved in October 1977 and have been received ever since. They consist of to-and-fro conversations, usually initiated by Dr Mueller when the machine was left running and sometimes carried on for considerable lengths. Meek only announced his breakthrough when he felt society was ready for it, and when he was prepared to market the apparatus for home testing. His announcement was carried in banner headlines by most of the psychic press, with featured articles about the research appearing in both *Psychic News* in Great Britain and in *New Realities* in the United States. Many researchers engaged in tape-recorded 'spirit' voice research (uncritically) heralded the Meek/O'Neill work as the long-awaited breakthrough.

I have known Mr Meek for some years, though not intimately and our meetings have been infrequent and casual. But I know him well enough to know that he is an honest and courageous man. But when I received a packet of information on his investigations I became very sceptical of the whole affair. The tapes of the voices which he provided me with were hardly impressive, and when I spoke over the phone with him, any hopes that there might possibly be something to the whole Spiricom business were dashed to pieces. The voices sounded exactly like the synthesized voices you can easily produce on a theramin, and they often used phraseology that exactly matched some of the idiosynchrasies in William O'Neill's own speech. That appeared awfully suspicious. I was also taken aback when George admitted to me that, in all the years he has worked with his engineer, he had never once heard the voices over Spiricom. O'Neill always heard and recorded them when he was alone. Of course, now that the whole Spiricom affair has become public, perhaps researchers such as myself could personally investigate O'Neill's claim and talk to the deceased Dr Mueller ourselves. But then I learned that contact with Dr Mueller had (suspiciously?) been lost right before Mr Meek had gone public.

In the light of these revelations, I see no reason to believe that William O'Neill's claimed contact with the voice of Dr Mueller is anything but a hoax, and that he has been pulling the wool over the eyes of his benefactor.

The Taped-Voice Phenomenon as Evidence for Survival

Are the voices that bona fide researchers have recorded really those of the dead? This is the real issue at stake. A great deal of evidence indicates that they are. For example, many experimenters working with the taped-voice phenomenon have occasionally been able to recognize the voices produced on their tapes. Jurgenson is sure that the first voice he ever recorded was that of his mother. Likewise, von Szalay has taped a voice speaking in Hungarian which both he and Raymond agree sounds just like his late father's. When Colin Smythe and Bander began their experiments, Bander identified the first whisper his colleague produced on tape as his mother's voice. Sometimes these voices will even call out their own names as though trying to identify themselves.

Another and very different explanation for the voices, however, has been offered by Dr Hans Bender, a German psychologist who heads a division of parapsychology at the University of Freiburg. Bender personally investigated both Jurgenson and Raudive and even made voice prints of their taped effects. These prints have not only proved that Jurgenson and Raudive have received *human* voices on tape, but that they usually picked up several voices in the course of a session. However, Bender does not believe that these articulations are actually produced by the dead. He argues that the 'voices' are probably psychokinetic phenomena masterminded by the unconscious minds of the experimenters themselves. In other words, he believes that Raudive, Jurgenson, and others have (or had) the ability to unconsciously project some sort of energy from their minds which is capable of manipulating magnetic impulses produced in the recording equipment. These psychic manipulations, in turn, form artificial voices on the electro-magnetic tape. Or perhaps, argues Bender, the mind directly imprints the 'voices' on the tape.

Of course, the crux of Bender's argument rests on one crucial issue. Are these taped effects produced by *paraphysical independent voices actually speaking into the microphone* but inaudible to the human ear? Or are they, as Bender suggests, psychokinetic effects imprinted *directly* on the tape or through the microphone? This question has prompted a number of researchers to explore the actual mechanics of the taped voices, and they have come up with a variety of solutions.

One of the first investigators to address himself to this problem was Raymond Bayless. Since Art can produce independent voices as well as taped voices, Raymond naturally theorized that the latter was merely a rarified form of the former. (Remember, Art's voices can sometimes be heard quite audibly over the loudspeaker even if he sits many feet from the microphone.) To test his theory, Raymond carried out a simple experiment. He conducted a series of short sessions with von Szalay during which he alternately left the microphone 'open' or blocked with heavy material. As he expected, Art could not produce taped-voices as long as the microphone was obstructed. This fact tends to indicate that Art cannot directly imprint voices on tape, but that somehow a human-like voice is actually speaking into the microphone when these taped effects are produced.[7]

Raymond's findings have been challenged, though, by two other investigators. Richard Sheargold, a British engineer and parapsychologist, is currently following up on some of Jurgenson's and Raudive's leads. He believes, unlike Bayless, that taped-voice effects are electronic in nature and occur when the random white noise taped over a radio — or produced by a tape machine itself when left running — is *re-ordered* by some psychic process in order to form meaningful words and sounds. Sheargold is now trying to demonstrate his theory by way of a series of experiments he is just completing. First he tapes a white noise band from a radio and then replays it to make sure no voices have been impressed on it. He then replays this white noise track through a microphone into another tape recorder while mentally trying to make contact with the 'voice entities'. Sheargold has found that several voices will become imprinted on the *second* tape during this procedure, and theorizes that somehow the white noise has been systematically rearranged to form them. His research would also seem to confirm Jurgenson's claim that sometimes human speech, when recorded, will be reorganized by the 'voice entities' and made to deliver meaningful words and messages.

Sheargold's experiment, though, is full of loopholes. It could be argued that these secondary voices are actually produced by some independent voice via the microphone during the re-recording process. So far, Sheargold has not refined his experiment in order to rule out this possibility.

The late William Welch, who was a well-known Hollywood scriptwriter before his recent death, also felt that taped-voice effects are electromagnetic in nature. Welch, who initiated his own investigations after first working with von Szalay, based his view on an oddity he ran into during one of his tape experiments in 1973. While replaying a taping session, he discovered a voice printed on a part of his tape which had not been run through the machine.

So just what are we supposed to conclude from these frequently contradictory findings? It seems obvious, at least to me, that the 'voice entities' (whether they are the dead or some lobotomized portion of our Ids) may use *any* procedure available to them while trying to place their voices on tape. They may not be limited to any one strategy. Some voices may be paraphysical productions, while others might well be psychokinetic and/or electromagnetic impressions. But of course, these findings still do not resolve the most important issue the taped-voice phenomenon raises: Are these voices those of the departed or merely the surreptitious psychic productions of our own minds?

Both possibilities are equally plausible. However, it is certainly interesting that all of those researchers most closely involved with the study of the taped-voice phenomenon — Raudive, Jurgenson, Welch, Seidl, Bayless and von Szalay — have come to believe that the voices emanate from the world of the dead. Only Sheargold has remained uncommitted. Even Professor Gebhard Frei, a Catholic theologian and parapsychologist who studied the Raudive work for many years before his own death, was forced to admit that, ' . . . everything I've read and heard forces me to the supposition that only the hypothesis of the voices belonging to transcendental personalities has any chance of explaining the full scope of these phenomena.'

But perhaps it is still too early to spend too much time wondering just *who* or *what* is producing these voices. In this respect, perhaps the most cogent remarks about the voice phenomenon were recently made by Dr Walter Uphoff, a retired college professor now engaged in taped-voice research in Wisconsin: 'My basic curiosity about the voices is that they are there . . . . at all. I want to know how they come to be there in the first place and how to stabilize the contact.'

Uphoff's queries may soon be answered. To date, taped-voice research is being conducted in the United States, Italy, Germany, Austria, and in most other European countries, by dozens of investigators. A breakthrough is bound to come. And when it does, perhaps the issues raised by such experimenters as Bayless, Sheargold, Welch, Raudive and others will finally be resolved at that time.

That breakthrough, in fact, may already have come. My own close connection with much of the research summarized in this chapter gradually led me to believe that this new research on electronic contact with the dead has a considerable bearing on a related phenomenon — a phenomenon so bizarre and unbelievable that I had to overcome several of my own biases in order to study it.

6.

Phone-Calls from the Dead?

Ronald Beard's wife had died. The date was March of an undesignated year in the 1960s and Beard, a writer by profession, had fled to Rome in an attempt to recover from the emotional trauma of his loss. But although his wife's body lay securely sealed in a British cemetery, Beard had not yet heard (quite literally) the last from her. The incident occurred one morning while he was still snoozing in his Rome hotel. The phone rang unexpectedly, and fumbling for the receiver, Beard was stunned to hear the voice of a long-distance operator announcing a person-to-person call from his wife! Moments later, a phantom voice began speaking over the line. It was his wife's voice all right, reciting the words of one of his own poems. The voice gradually faded away until only silence could be heard over the receiver.

This little scenario plays a key role in Anthony Burgess's novel, *Beard's Roman Women*, written in 1976. Burgess, better known as the author of *A Clockwork Orange* and *Earthly Powers*, structures his novel around the central character's dilemma in the face of a series of phantom phone-calls from his deceased wife.[1] The book is lively and colourful, but it's a novel nonetheless. Or is it?

When I first learned about Burgess's book I was intrigued. Having finished several years of work on the 'tape-recorded spirit voice' controversy, Raymond Bayless and I were beginning to take more seriously all those reports we had heard — and dismissed — from people who steadfastly believe that they have indeed received phone calls from the dead. So of course Burgess's novel prompted me to wonder if the experiences of 'Ronald Beard' were totally fictional, or if Burgess had modelled them on an incident he had heard about. Or perhaps, I thought, they might even be based on a personal experience. I wrote to Burgess. Several weeks passed before, in a brief note mailed from his home in Monaco, Burgess confirmed my suspicions. Yes, he admitted, the psychic phone-calls had occurred to him just as reported in the novel. In fact, the novel was actually a sort of disguised autobiography. Burgess also described the bizarre series of phone-calls as a 'damned nuisance', revealing the same sort of personal ambivalance about the psychic contacts as 'Beard' feels in the novel.

Despite Burgess's rather cynical attitude about the calls he received from his deceased wife, most people who have received 'phone-calls from the dead' report reactions ranging from awe to shock. It is probably for this reason that few people ever report these calls to parapsychologists. So it was quite a surprise when I discovered, as I began collecting more and more cases of these 'phone-calls from the dead', just how common — and diversified — they can be.

Researching 'Phone-Calls from the Dead'

I first heard about these phantom calls several years ago, in 1967, when I first entered the field of parapsychology. An acquaintance of mine told me about a friend of her's who had once received a most enigmatic call. The woman claimed that the caller spoke in the *exact* voice of her deceased son who had been killed in a motorcycle accident a couple of months before. The voice had only spoken his mother's name and offered his own before the line went dead.

At the time I really didn't take this little story too seriously. It struck me as little different from dozens of other 'tall stories'. However, over the next ten years, I came across more and more of these reports — and found myself totally incapable of explaining them, or explaining them away.

For instance, in April of 1977, my colleague and friend, Raymond Bayless, received a call from a Dr John Medved, a prominent Los Angeles physician. By the time he contacted us, he had called several parapsychologists hoping to find someone who could help him understand the strange drama in which he had participated. Raymond assured Dr Medved that we had indeed heard of people receiving phone-calls from the dead, and perhaps put more at ease by this candid admission, the doctor related his experience to us in some detail.

The episode had occurred in July 1974, a few days after his mother's death. She had always wanted to be buried in the family's home town in Idaho, and Medved had travelled there to help with the funeral arrangements. The day after his return home he received a phone-call from her at six-thirty in the morning: 'It was exactly 6.30 and I thought that it was no time for my exchange to be bothering me', Medved explained to us. He jumped out of bed and scurried to a desk phone in his hallway by which he always keeps a pad and pencil. 'When I said "Hello!" ' he continued, 'the voice on the phone said "Johnny". It was a little odd sounding, and I thought it was one of my sisters. It sounded a little dismayed, as if she was calling to report a problem.'

Our witness asked the caller if there was a problem, but the voice only repeated his name, drawing out its enunciation eerily: 'John-n-n-n-y-y-y,' it said. As Medved went on to tell us:

I again said, 'What's the matter? Who is this?' I don't know whether the voice said 'Johnny' again, but then I began to get rather excited. The next thing the voice said was, 'Is that you, Johnny dear?' By this time I didn't know if someone was pulling a joke on me or what, and my voice really got high. 'What's the matter?' I said. 'Who is this?' I kept repeating this, and the voice said, 'Your mother.'

After concluding his bizarre story, Dr Medved explained to us that the voice spoke in the *exact* timbre of his mother's! There could be no mistake about it. Dr Medved also gave us the name of a house guest to whom he had related the experience right after the call had come through. We tracked down this witness, and he indeed was able to tell us that Dr Medved had told him about the bizarre call and that he had seemed visibly shaken by it.

Of course, if you're a cynic at heart you might want merely to dismiss Dr Medved's call as a hoax. Maybe someone who knew him, knew about his bereavement, had imitated his mother's voice over the line in order to play a cruel and somewhat twisted joke. But how can you explain a phantom phone-call in which the voice not only speaks in the exact timbre of a deceased person, but also uses phrases or imparts a message typical of that person?

One case of this sort, in which I was able to talk to the witness at some length three years after the incident, was sent to me by a housewife in Oklahoma, Mrs Mary Meredith, who had seen me on a TV interview talking about incidents of this type. She was still nervous about telling her strange story to anyone, but eventually sent me a complete report of an incident that had occurred right after an operation she had undergone in 1977. Here's the story as Mrs Meredith first told it:

I had surgery on the 22nd of August, 1977. I came home a week later, and of course, I had plenty of mail waiting for me. One was a letter from my mother, who lives in Kentucky, telling of my cousin Shirley's death. She lived in Louisville, Kentucky. The phone rang when I was in the kitchen, so I answered it and this voice came over the line and said, 'Hi Mary, this is Shirley Jean.' I asked 'Who' and the voice said again, 'This is Shirley Jean.' The voice was so much like my cousin's voice, who spoke with a soft southern accent. Then of course I just went to pieces. I thought it was really her at first and then I knew it couldn't be. So I answered with, 'What kind of a person are you? Are you sick? What kind of a person would pull something like this on anyone?' Then I hung up the phone.

I was so upset that I went up and laid on the bed. But then the phone rang again, and I pulled myself together and answered. The same voice came on the phone and I said, 'I want to know who this is.' And the voice said, 'Mary, this is Shirley Jean. Are you all right?'

I tried to keep my head and said, 'Yes, how did you know that I had been sick?' And she answered, 'I was in the hospital with you.' I said she couldn't have been, and she replied that she was.

All the time I was talking — both times — I could hear her loud at times and then her voice seemed to fade away. I was very unnerved by all of this. Then my cousin said, 'Mary, I will call you again.' There seemed to be static or something on the phone and that was all there was to the incident. She just faded away.

I got to thinking about it afterward. I knew that no one in Oklahoma knew I had a cousin named Shirley Jean or any of my cousins up there in Kentucky. All my relatives lived in Kentucky. So I just tried to pass it off as something weird happening to me.

Mrs Meredith didn't think any more of the incident until she saw the television interview in which I described the work Raymond and I were engaged in. Finding someone to whom she could talk was a relief to her, so she contacted me. When I met Mrs Meredith some months later, she confirmed that she and her cousin had been very close and that there was no way she could have misidentified the voice on the phone. She also acknowledged that the phone-call came in — significantly enough — *at the very time she was reading of her cousin's death.* This very impressive and meaningful 'coincidence' couldn't possibly have come about by chance. It showed some sort of awareness or purpose on the part of the caller.

Another striking case was told to us by a noted Hollywood actress who gave us the story in confidence and asked us not to reveal her identity. The incident had occurred when Miss Adams (as we'll call her here) was 8 years old and living in Texas. That Thanksgiving, she and her family were having a holiday get-together at the home of a family friend. The occasion was somewhat marred, though, by the fact that two years earlier the friend's daughter had been killed in a car accident while away at college. Thanksgiving was a day on which she invariably returned home briefly. Everyone was apparently having a good time, nonetheless, when the phone rang. Miss Adams answered it. As she told us:

I . . . heard the long-distance operator say, 'I have a collect call.' She mentioned the name of my mother's friend and she mentioned the name of the daughter.

[In other words, the call was addressed to the friend, and the operator told Miss Adams that the call was from the deceased daughter.] This threw me a little bit even as a child, and I said, 'Just a minute.' I went and got my mother's friend. She came to the phone. I stood watching her, because I had heard the name and thought that maybe somebody was playing a joke on me or her or something. She listened on the phone, turned absolutely white, and fainted.

Later on I heard what happened. There was a great hushing up about it, but I learned that she had heard her daugher — who had been dead two or three years — speak to her. She said the same thing she always did before she came home: 'Mommie, it's me,' she said. 'I need twenty dollars to get home.'

The mother always sent her twenty dollars for good luck. She said she recognized the voice. They called the phone company, but they had no record of any phone call.

The fact that this alleged collect long-distance call was *not* billed to the family is a disturbing feature of this case. It indicates that these calls are not 'normal' phone-calls in the literal sense of the word. In other words, they do not seem to be monitored to the witnesses' phones by way of a central phone exchange. This is the route all normal calls between two parties are processed by the telephone company. Instead, it appears as though the calls are placed by manipulating the *specific phone on which the call is received.*

This phenomenon is best illustrated by a case we collected from a middle-aged Ohio man who had witnessed one of these phantom phone-calls when he was a child living on a small farm with his grandmother. Since the farm phone was often used by many of the local residents without permission, our witness's grandmother had it disconnected one day. The next evening, however, the phone rang. It was a long-distance call from a family friend in West Virginia saying that 'everything would be all right,' that she was 'going away' and that the witness 'would hear further within a few days'.

'Her voice seemed hollow,' our witness told us, 'and had a faraway manner about it.'

Naturally, our witness's grandmother was perplexed by the call and immediately contacted the local phone company to complain that the instrument had not been disconnected as she had requested. 'The lineman came out in the evening,' our witness explained. 'He pointed out to my grandmother the new white wire that was wound around the pole and not connected. Then he went up to the house and pointed out that the wire there was also disconnected.'

The upshot of this weird and seemingly 'impossible' call came, as predicted by the voice, a few days later when a letter arrived announcing the death of the family friend. She had died at the very time the call had been made.

This phenomenon, where the call comes in at the approximate time of the phantom caller's actual death, cropped up in several of our cases ... even those coming from countries other than the United States. This indicates that some of the patterns we have been isolating are universal to the 'phone-calls from the dead' phenomenon.

Reports Collected by Other Researchers

At the beginning of October 1980, two colleagues of ours wrote to us about their research into the psychic experiences reported by Italy's general public. Dr G. M. Rinaldi and his wife, of Bolzano, Italy, had started to come across phone-call cases very similar to the ones we had been collecting in this country since 1977. He and his wife had personally looked into the case of Mrs Emma Portocalschi of Turin, Italy, who had received a phantom phone-call on 18 August 1977. The woman told the investigators that her husband had died on that very date of cancer of the pancreas. His death occurred at four in the morning, so she was back home when the call came in at seven. She had not yet gone to bed and was fully awake and alert when the phone rang. Her husband's voice came on the line immediately. 'Emma,' it asked in a perplexed tone, 'why are you still home? I am waiting for you.' The poor woman was so shocked that she hung up the phone, only to regret her impulsive action later. The significance of the call lies in the fact that she had made it a habit to visit and help the nurse with her husband at seven every morning during the course of his hospitalization. Note again how the messages received during these calls, no matter how brief, are meaningful to both the caller and the witness.

Could someone have been playing a cruel joke on Mrs Portocalschi? This seems unlikely. Dr Rinaldi explained to us in his report on the case that the witness '. . . asserts that she heard a clear, normal voice, unmistakably the voice of her husband. She was alone at home and nobody was present who would be speaking and disturbing her hearing at the phone.'

Admittedly, all the phantom phone-calls cited so far have been rather banal. The voices have not been able to speak more than a few words, and what they had to say hardly seemed very enlightening, either. However, not all phone-calls from the dead are so fragmented. Sometimes a to-and-fro conversation will result, and the whole conversation will strike the witness as perfectly normal. These calls can go on for well over half an hour. They are, however, much rarer than the brief types of interaction cited in the above cases; but they represent a formidable aspect of the phantom phone-call mystery, and one that cannot be ignored.

Our best case of this sort was not directly collected by us, but was first published by Susy Smith in her book, *The Power of the Mind*. Miss Smith, a noted author of several books on the paranormal, personally interviewed the two witnesses who spoke to the phantom voice. The witnesses, Bonnie and C. E. MacConnell of Tucson, Arizona, even provided Miss Smith with a notarized statement about the incident. (Both have since died.) The case is somewhat involved.

The MacConnells had long had a family friend named Enid Johlson, who was an author and philanthropist. Unfortunately, by the time old age had set in, Enid's generosity had taken an undeserved toll of her resources. Having given away so much money, she found herself totally incapable of handling the medical bills that were resulting from the breakdown in her health. The result of her predicament was as might be expected. She ended up being shoved from one hospital to another. Her only hope was that she might be able to get another book written, an idea which the MacConnells heartily endorsed. The book, however, was never written, and the MacConnells eventually lost touch with her.

Several months later, on a Sunday evening in 1971, the MacConnells heard from Enid once again when a call came in from her. They were surprised to hear from her, and also surprised by the fact that her voice sounded youthful and vibrant — like the Enid of twenty years before. Enid explained that she had been transferred to the Handmaker Jewish Nursing Home in Tucson. Mrs MacConnell remembered during the course of their conversation that Enid's birthday was only a few days away, and she offered to bring her a bottle of wine as a present. 'I don't need it now,' was the voice's reply. Enid continued on about the quality of the care she was receiving, about the book she had not completed, and finally admitted that she had 'never been happier'. The entire conversation, in which both the MacConnells took part, lasted some thirty minutes.

On Friday of that same week, Mrs MacConnell decided to call Enid back, so she called up the Handmaker Nursing Home. That's when the shock came. The operator in charge of the switchboard explained that Enid Johlson had died the previous Sunday at 10.30 a.m. That was several hours *before* the MacConnells received her call. There could be no mistake about the time of the death, yet no error about the time of the mysterious call either.[2]

Exploring the Nature of the Calls
When we started coming across similar cases of extended phantom phone-calls, we were at first puzzled by them. Why, for instance, should

they be so rare? The MacConnell case is only one of about half a dozen of these prolonged calls that we've been able to collect. We were also curious as to why these phantom callers, such as Mrs Johlson, *never* mentioned anything about their own deaths. These phone-entities often seem to deliberately lead the witnesses to believe that they are living, breathing people. Again, the Johlson-MacConnell case is typical in this respect. 'Enid' did not admit that she was dead, yet nevertheless put a dampener on Mrs MacConnell's suggestion that they get together on her birthday.

The answers to these questions only came some months after we started seriously collecting phantom phone-call cases. The clue came when we noted that the MacConnells *did not know* that Enid Johlson was dead when they received her call. In this respect the case stands in striking contrast to the ones reported to us by Dr Medved and Patricia Adams. In these instances, the witnesses were fully aware that they had suddenly been placed in direct communication with the dead. With this clue in mind, we began to re-evaluate all the cases in our files (over fifty by this time) and found a fairly consistent pattern which differentiated the fragmentary from the prolonged 'death calls' we had amassed. If the witness knows that he is talking to a deceased entity, the calls will invariably be short and abortive. But, if the witness does not know that he is receiving a phantom phone-call, the conversation can go on for up to thirty minutes.

The case we received from Mary Meredith threw us a bit. This was reported after we had finished our analysis. This case did not seem to fit the type of brief exchanges we noted when the witness knows the caller is dead, though it wasn't a very extended call either. It may have been prolonged since Mrs Meredith virtually fought against acknowledging that the call came from the dead.

The pattern that we uncovered about the length of these calls can readily explain why in cases of prolonged telephonic contact these phantom voices never 'let on' about their own deaths. It seems reasonable to assume that phone calls from the dead can only occur when several psychic factors come into play within the minds of the caller and the witness. For example, all of the witnesses whose cases we've quoted were in a passive frame of mind — sleeping, just waking, relaxing at home in the evening, and so forth — when their calls came through. In other words, our witnesses were relaxed, both mentally and physically, when the calls were received. This factor may have helped make the psychic contact possible in the first place. Parapsychologists have long known that mental states typified by relaxation and freedom from preoccupation are ESP-conducive. This may be true of the state of mind one must enter before a phone-call from the dead can take place as well. The reason why most phone calls from the dead are so short may stem from the fact that the witness usually becomes very agitated when he or she realizes what is happening. This mental agitation may destroy the psychic conditions which have made the contact possible to begin with.

Now this agitation would not occur in those instances in which the witness did not know that the caller was deceased. So, they may go on for several minutes. Our phantom callers may, therefore, deliberately withhold information pertaining to their own deaths so that their psychic contacts can be prolonged. In one of our cases, in fact, the call came to a halt at the moment the witness tried to encourage the caller to admit to her own death.

I learned of this case from the witnesses, Mr and Mrs Joe Bonneau, very shortly after it had occurred, so the incident was fresh in their minds when they reported it to me. It had occurred on a Sunday afternoon, 18 November 1979 at their home in Portland, Oregon. Mrs Bonneau was in the kitchen preparing for a big Thanksgiving dinner that afternoon while Mr Bonneau, who took the call, was sitting at the dining room table making some phone-calls. The first hint that something unusual was about to happen came when the phone emitted a short abortive ring. No subsequent ringings followed, but Mr Bonneau impulsively picked up the phone anyway . . . even after waiting several seconds. What he heard excited him tremendously. His dead sister's voice came over the phone, asking for him. Before he could even get his wits about him, he asked his sister how she was. The following brief conversation followed:

'I am fine, is that you Joe?' the voice answered.

'Yes, this is Joe. Who are you?' was Mr Bonneau's surprised response. The voice answered by giving her proper name: 'I am Mary.'

At this moment Mr Bonneau realized what was happening to him. 'Oh God,' he said, 'it is good to hear your voice. Where are you? What are you doing?'

But at this point some static came over the line. The witness explained to the voice that he couldn't hear her, but the voice only replied 'I know. I have to go, but I do want to talk to you.' The voice faded out, but didn't hang up. Mr Bonneau only replaced the receiver back on the hook when it seemed that no further conversation would be forthcoming. Mr Bonneau later explained that the voice was clear and full, but as soon as he tried to get the voice to explain where it was calling from and further identify itself, the static interrupted the call. Mr Bonneau remains totally convinced that the voice was that of his sister and was easily recognizable. But even at present he had remained intrigued about why the phone only rang once . . . and why he picked it up after it had discontinued.*

Our theory that these calls are often aborted because of the witness's growing shock and excitement is admittedly hypothetical and somewhat after-the-fact. But it does explain just why there seem to be two different types of phone-call from the dead, and why the latter only occur when the witnesses remain in the dark about the nature of the calls. Had Mrs MacConnell not called the Handmaker Jewish Nursing Home a few days after Enid had called, she may have never realized that she had taken part in a remarkable psychic manifestation.

Problems in the Evidence

How can we be sure that these 'phone-calls from the dead' really are coming from the dead, and not from some other source? This may strike you as a rather odd question, but it is an important one. There are actually two very different possible explanations for these phantom phone-calls. The first is simply that the dead can, on occasion, make contact with the living by manipulating electromagnetic equipment. But there is another possible explanation as well. Could it be that, through the powers of our own minds, *we* are producing these calls ourselves?

We know that the mind possesses remarkable psychokinetic (or 'mind over matter') abilities. It has the power to move physical objects, levitate tables, heal the sick, and — according to recent findings — produce poltergeist attacks. And sometimes we can employ these abilities unconsciously. A poltergeist, for example, seems to occur when someone in a disturbed family starts using mind-over-matter unconsciously in order to produce all sorts of 'ghostly' disturbances. Furniture moves about of its own accord, banging sounds break out, objects appear and disappear mysteriously in the house. If this 'agent' is removed from the family or goes to sleep, the haunting will stop. Yet this person rarely realizes that he or she is actually producing the phenomena, since the poltergeist is being masterminded by some portion of the mind buried deep within the unconscious.

In the light of the fact that we all possess innate psychokinetic abilities, there is a real possibility that our own minds might have the ability to electromagnetically and psychically manipulate a telephone system and produce a phantom phone-call.

Perhaps this idea does seem far-fetched, but there is even some evidence that we, the living, can produce phantom phone-calls on occasion. I can vouch for this fact from personal experience, since I once produced

*We have actually collected several cases in which these bizzare calls are heralded by strange rings of one sort or another.

one of these calls myself. The incident occurred in 1975. It was four o'clock on a bright Thursday afternoon, and I was lying on my living room couch thinking about making a phone-call to a psychologist I knew at the U.C.L.A. Neuropsychiatric Institute. Although I intended to make the call, I never did. At about six that evening, though, I got the shock of my life when a call came in from the Institute and from the office of the very psychologist I had thought about calling. The call was from her research assistant saying that he was 'answering my message'. When I asked what in blazes he was talking about, he told me that at 4.00 p.m. a call had come in to them from me. The caller had left my name, and had asked that the call be returned! A volunteer worker had answered the phone and had taken down the message.

I didn't know what to make of this experience in 1975, since that was a bit before I began to get seriously interested in the phantom phone-call mystery. But as I began studying 'phone-calls from the dead', I started running into several cases almost identical to my own. One such incident was reported to me by Jerome Clark, the associate editor of *Fate* magazine and a friend of mine:

> The incident occurred one Saturday afternoon in June 1975. A friend, Dr Benton Jamison, and I were sitting in my apartment in Moorhead, Minnesota, and conversing. The phone rang. I answered it. The person on the other end, whose voice I immediately recognized, identified herself as Mary, a friend of my wife's. My wife Penny baby-sat Mary's two young sons from time to time, and Mary asked if she would do so that evening because she wanted to go out. I explained that Penny was out of town visiting her parents and wouldn't be back until the next day. Mary expressed disappointment, and that was the end of the conversation.

When Jerry's wife returned home she was told about the call and phoned Mary right away. 'Mary was flabbergasted', Jerry wrote, 'and denied she had made any such call. She said, however, that she'd thought about doing so all afternoon but had decided against it. When Penny explained that the telephone 'Mary' had expressed disappointment, the real Mary said she would never have done that. I agree. At the time of the phone exchange, in fact, I had been a little surprised at her reaction.'

Dr Jamison personally corroborated the entire episode.

In the light of these 'intention cases', as we've come to call them, we cannot automatically assume that phone-calls from the dead are what they seem to be. *If* a living person can produce a phantom voice resembling his own over a distant phone system, it seems at least theoretically possible that we might be able to create the voices of the dead over our own phones as well. When Raymond Bayless and I first began our study of 'phone-calls from the dead', we really didn't think we would be able to resolve this issue. Nonetheless, as we collected more and more accounts, we found that they were supplying clues about the nature of 'phone-calls from the dead' which indicated that these calls are, indeed, initiated by the dead, and not by some unconscious use of psychic power by the living.

Phone-Calls from the Dead and the Case for Survival

To begin with, most of these phantom calls are made to people who know their callers are dead. Many of our cases only occurred after the caller had been dead six months or longer. A full 22 per cent of our cases fell into this category. It seems to us that there would be practically no psychological reason why a person would be unconsciously motivated to produce such a phantom phone-call after so long an interval. Other cases, by contrast were similar to the one our Ohio correspondent reported, where the call had come at the very time the caller was undergoing her own death. We speculated that, in these instances, the witness had unconsciously received a telepathic message about the death, and had psychokinetically produced a 'death call' as a means of bringing this information to his conscious attention. But this theory just cannot explain why such a large proportion of 'phone-calls from the dead' are produced months after the death of the caller, and when *only* the dead person would have any motivation for producing such contact.

Another clue about the source of the calls came when we realized that the dead have a certain penchant for calling on days which had (or have) psychological significance for either themselves or their living friends or relatives. A full 10 per cent of our cases occurred on emotionally meaningful days.

One of our most striking cases of this phenomenon was reported to us by Mrs Mary Cahill, a New York housewife who received a phone-call from her dead daughter on Mother's Day in 1943. This was six months after the girl had died. Mrs Cahill had previously reported the incident to *Fate* magazine, but we were able to get an independent account of the episode. The call had occurred that evening while Mrs Cahill was relaxing and listening to a radio programme. The voice, which she immediately recognized as her dead daughter's, could only blurt out, 'Hello, Mom! How are you? Can you hear me? Hello, Mom?' After that, the line became clogged by the mumblings of several additional voices. Mrs Cahill could hear her daughter's voice through the static asking if she could be heard, and then the line went silent.

These 'anniversary' cases suggest that the calls may not be chance affairs, but *carefully planned communications* masterminded by the callers themselves. These calls also indicate a definite awareness and motivation though this may apply as much to the person receiving the call as to the caller.

Mrs Cahill's account is also interesting since she heard several miscellaneous voices talking over the line when her phantom call came through. This is a feature which crops up now and then, though not often, in several of our accounts. This odd phenomenon may also indicate that these calls emanate from the world of the dead. It seems plausible that, if some channel between the living and the dead has been opened, many intelligences might try to make contact over it. At the same time, there seems no reason why, if a living person produces an imaginary call, he should 'pollute' it with interference from additional phantom voices.

Our study of 'phone-calls from the dead' is still in its infancy. We certainly cannot claim that we have solved the many mysteries presented by these enigmatic contacts. We don't know, for instance, exactly how the calls are made, who is most prone to receive them, and when they are likely to occur. But one thing is certain: these calls are not as rare as you might think. Cases have been reported all the way back to the 1920s, and more and more people are willing to place their experiences on record. Unfortunately, to date, few parapsychologists have been prepared to study this incredible phenomenon. Indeed, it may well strike most of them as just a little *too* bizarre for comfort, though they are certainly no more peculiar than any other type of psychic manifestation.

7.

Reincarnation Reconsidered

Of all the many conceptions of an afterlife that have come down to us since time immemorial, reincarnation is perhaps the most perennial. Many primitive cultures accept the doctrine and today it is best exemplified in the teachings of several oriental religions.

By tradition, research into the reincarnation question has been subsumed within the survival issue in general. The idea that we each possess a soul, and that it can reappear on the earth through some sort of transmigration, represents a specific *form* of survival after death. Whether this process is a universal law, or merely occurs by the choice or the will of the deceased individual, is not really a crucial point. What *is* important is that reincarnation entails the survival of our memories and personality beyond physical death, even if in a different conceptual framework from that to which we are accustomed. The evidence for reincarnation also directly implies a more conventional state of personal survival for at least a limited duration. In the cases that will be summarized in this chapter, months or even years often passed between the death of the original personality and his or her purported 'reincarnation'. This lengthy span of time certainly implies that some sort of personal survival occurred during the hiatus.

Reincarnation is not, therefore, a doctrine inherently opposed to the idea of personal survival. On the contrary, the evidence implies that such a state of existence necessarily precedes it. Reincarnation is therefore an inherent and important part of the survival issue.

Until recently, reincarnation was regarded by most Westerners as an exotic concept associated with certain non-Christian religions, notably Hinduism and Buddhism. Of late, however, ordinary people in the West who have never heard of the concept have reported 'reincarnation' experiences.

For example, the following letter was sent to me from a young woman in Virginia who had no previous belief in reincarnation but came to believe in it as a result of her direct personal experience. Reincarnation to her is not an abstract doctrine to which she subscribes as an act of faith, but a living reality.

One day in 1971 she and a friend were driving from Patterson, New Jersey, to Baltimore. She had just moved to New Jersey from Tennessee and had never visited the state before.

> We were driving down the New Jersey Turnpike, and I felt very strange, all the landscape was very familiar to me . . . I turned to Joanne, and said, 'You know, I have never been here before, but I believe about a mile or so down the road, is a house I used to live in.'
>
> As we went down the turnpike (heading North), everything was familiar . . . the older houses, and I began describing *what* we would see before we came to it.
>
> Approximately three miles or so passed, and I told my friend, that around the bend, we would come to a small town; it was set very close to the turnpike. I told her that the houses would be white frame, two storey homes, rather close together . . . and that I felt that I lived there when I was six years old or so, and that I used to sit with my 'granny' on the front porch. The memories overwhelmed me, and I could remember sitting on the swing, on the front porch, and my grandmother buttoning up my high-topped shoes. I could not do it myself. When we got to the town, I recognized the house immediately, only the front porch swing was not there . . . however, at the time I lived there with my Granny, I told my friend, I *remembered* sitting there, and also that my Granny used to walk two blocks down the street with me, to a drug store, and there was a high marble counter, white, and we used to get lemonade from the drug store, and I liked to go there. As we drove down the little street, I took her to the drug store, or where it *used* to be. It was still there, or rather, the building was still there, much the same as it used to look, but it was boarded up, and we could not look inside.

What could have been a dramatic dénouement to the incident was rather spoiled by her friend's growing uneasiness with what was transpiring. But the story has an uncanny ending nonetheless:

> As we stood there, I 'knew' that I had died when I was about 6 or 7 years old . . . and I tried to get Joanne to let me direct her to the cemetery where 'I' was buried, but she was so frightened that she would not take the drive. As we were leaving the town, I told her, 'In about three blocks, there is a small hill, rolling, and the cemetery is *there*, and that is where they buried me.' It was true . . . the cemetery *was* there, and as I had described it.
>
> We got on the turnpike again, and went on to Patterson . . . and I still know that once, around the early 1900s that I lived there, and died there.

What is so impressive about this account is that it is *veridical*: the experiences imparted information that could not possibly have already been lodged in the witness's memory.

Reports such as the case quoted above are apparently not rare, although no academic parapsychologists have ever bothered to study this body of reincarnation evidence. Research on spontaneous past-life memory only came to public attention in 1979 when Dr Frederick Lenz, a psychologist in San Diego, published his book *Lifetimes*, in which he published and analysed a large number of similar incidents.[1] He has collected over a hundred, and has found that spontaneous past-life memory tends to occur in dreams, during meditation, via *déjà vu* experiences and as waking visions. These waking vision cases are the most characteristic. The experiencer usually feels as though he has been literally transported in time back to his or her past life. Lenz, too, has found that some of his cases are veridical. The following is a typical case from his files which was reported by a young woman in San Diego. She was a teenager at the time of the incident:

It happened when I was just seventeen. I was at home, baby-sitting for my little sister. My parents had gone out to celebrate their wedding anniversary. I was in the kitchen cooking dinner when I heard a loud ringing sound in my head. It got louder and louder until I was very frightened. The sound did not come from outside me, but from within. The room began to shift and fade, and I thought I was going to pass out. The next thing I remember, I was standing on a cliff overlooking the sea. I was watching the waves roll in and break on the rocks far below me. I heard the pounding surf and smelled the salt air. I turned around and began to walk through a field that was behind me. The sun was out and I felt warm and happy. I was returning to my flock of sheep that I had left up at the pasture. As I walked I sang a favorite song until I reached the crest of the hill. I thought about many Greek towns that I would like to one day visit. I sat down near the sheep and, all alone, rocked back and forth singing. Then the vision ended, and I was back in my kitchen.

I didn't know what to make of what happened to me, and I figured that I had had some kind of vivid daydream. However, several years later when I was on vacation from college, I went to Europe, and one of the countries I visited was Greece. I was very much attracted to some of the small coastal cities. One day while motoring with friends we came to a stretch of road that overlooked the sea. I was filled with a number of conflicting emotions, but one thing was clear: I wanted to get out of the car. I asked my friends to stop for a minute; they pulled over to the side of the road overlooking the sea and looked down. As I did I saw the exact scene I had seen several years before in my vision in the kitchen. I turned around and walked away from the car and my friends. I walked with a purpose, as if I knew the way. I followed a path through a field and began to ascend an embankment. When

I reached the top and looked around, I recognized the spot where I had been with the sheep in my vision. It was exactly as I had remembered it. I was filled with memories of places and scenes, and I knew I had returned 'home' again. Although it made no sense, I felt that I had lived there in another time. I returned to my friends in the car and explained my sensation to them. They didn't seem to understand what I was saying, and I finally gave up trying to explain to them.

But Lenz's work has not merely entailed collecting such incidents. He has also analysed them in great detail and feels that, as a result of his research, he has uncovered a pattern to which these cases conform. He suggests that people who are about to remember their past lives go through a 'phenomenological syndrome' which culminates in the emergence of the past-life memory. First the subject tends to feel his body becoming lighter, and vivid colours begin to dance before his eyes. A mood of euphoria or even ecstasy will then overwhelm the witness and the room will vibrate. The past-life recall finally emerges at this point and the subject will usually find himself transported in time to a scene from his past-life. The scene will last only a few moments before fading. He will then find himself back in the twentieth century, perhaps feeling as though he has emerged from a trance. Dr Lenz does not say that this progressive phenomenology accompanies *all* such past-life recall, but that *elements* of this syndrome tend to accompany most such incidents.

Had Lenz isolated a specific reincarnation syndrome, similar to Moody's isolation of the near-death encounter syndrome? (See Chapter 3.) If the 'Lenz effect' was a real part of the reincarnation experience, it should be easy to replicate his findings. So I decided to conduct this much-needed replication. I began by writing letters to two national magazines that publish material on the paranormal, asking readers to send me details of any reincarnation experiences they may have had. From the replies I was able to cull about twenty solid cases of spontaneous past-life recall. The majority of my correspondents sent in dream cases, while several others were waking vision cases. A few *déjà vu* reports were also filed.

The results of my study were mixed. I was able to collect many cases that precisely matched the type of cases Lenz had reported, especially those odd 'waking vision' accounts. At least five contained veridical evidence: that is, information was communicated in the dream or vision which was later verified. One correspondent dreamt of dying at the hands of Viking invaders, and later discovered that Norse leaders wore the exact type of ring she had seen her 'husband' wearing before he, too, was killed. Another man had extreme *déjà vu* experiences while reading about General Custer's career and later verified through subsequent reading many of the 'facts' that had come into his mind intuitively. However, I did not find any cases which fitted the 'Lenz effect.' Perhaps my sample was too small to reveal such a pattern, or perhaps Lenz collected his cases in such a way that he biased his witnesses into tailoring their accounts to fit a spurious pattern that he felt was emerging in his data. Whatever the case, more systematic research is needed to resolve the issue.

Despite the unanswered questions relating to my research, I was sufficiently impressed with the quality of the cases I collected to re-evaluate my views on reincarnation. Unfortunately, the problem is that these accounts seldom contain much verifiable information. They are brief and ephemeral phenomena, and a sceptic could dismiss them as hallucinations or delusions. Certainly the work of Dr Lenz and my own attempted replication should be viewed only within the larger context of ongoing research into the reincarnation question.

Extracerebral Memory

The greatest single body of evidence supporting the reincarnation doctrine has been collected by Dr Ian Stevenson, a psychiatrist and para-psychologist at the University of Virginia, who has been collecting cases of 'extracerebral memory' since the 1960s. Extracerebral memory is a fancy term that refers to those cases in which an individual, usually a child, seems to recall having experienced a past life. Not only do these people recall previous lives, but sometimes they are able to discuss them in great detail and accuracy, even when they speak of having lived in foreign cultures and during many different historical periods. To date, Stevenson has published no less than four books examining those cases which he has personally investigated.

Roughly, the types of evidence that Stevenson has collected fall into two general categories. First are cases in which the child merely remembers a past life, and several scattered details about it. In the second category are instances wherein the child has apparently inherited traits or physical characteristics from his previous incarnation. Most commonly, for example, such a child will be born with physical deformities or birthmarks which correspond to similar marks possessed by the original person.

The case of Indika Guneratne, a Sri Lankan boy born in 1962, is typical of a simple 'past-life recall' case. Stevenson began his investigation into the case in 1968 and published his findings in 1974 in the A.S.P.R. *Journal.* [2]

Indika first began to speak when he was about two years old, and a year or so later began describing a past life as a wealthy resident of Matara, a city on the south coast of Sri Lanka. Among his recollections were those of the beautiful home he had owned, a Mercedes Benz he possessed, as well as memories of his estates and pet elephants. Indika's father, G. D. Guneratne, looked into his son's claims and discovered that a wealthy man who fitted his son's descriptions had indeed lived in Matara. But the elder Guneratne never pursued the investigation further. This was that job that Stevenson took upon himself when he visited India and Sri Lanka on a field investigation. Stevenson was able to substantiate a great many of the statements Indika had made, and which his father had carefully recorded. These incidents seemed to correspond to the life of a wealthy lumber merchant, a Mr K. G. J. Weerasinghe, an elephant owner who lived in Matara and who died in 1960. Among these were the pertinent facts that, in his past life, Indika claimed that he was wealthy, that his home was by a railway station, that he had a servant named Premdasa, owned several elephants, and had engaged in a serious altercation with his brother-in-law.

By making several inquiries in Matara, Stevenson substantiated most of Indika's claims. But there were a few errors to be considered as well. Weerasinghe had only owned one elephant, not many, nor had he owned a Mercedes. Oddly, though, Indika was even able to recall the car's registration number. Upon checking, Stevenson discovered that such a registration number had been issued for a Mercedes, but that the car had been owned by a gentleman living in a town neighbouring Matara! But considering how fallible and capricious human memory can be, the few inaccuracies which marred Indika's recollections do not materially detract from the overall evidentiality of the case.

Despite these inaccuracies, Indika's memories were about 90 per cent accurate when applied to the life and death of K. G. J. Weerasinghe. His most outstanding piece of information was correctly recalling the specific name of his previous servant, Premdasa, who had been Weerasinghe's chauffeur.

Even more evidential than simple 'past-life recall' cases are those instances in which a child is born with some sort of mark or deformity which seems related to his previous life. Stevenson has encountered a number of such instances. Perhaps the most fascinating is the strange case of Corliss Chotkin, Jr, an Alaskan Indian who was born in 1948 and who recalled a previous life as a distant relative, Victor Vincent, who died in 1946.[3] During his life, Vincent, being a full-blooded Tlinget Indian, accepted reincarnation as a matter of course, since it is a belief widespread among his tribe. Shortly before his death, in fact, he told his niece that, should he die soon, he would voluntarily reincarnate as her son. Corliss Chotkin, Jr was born only eighteen months after Vincent's death. And if we take the case at face value, Vincent made good his prediction. Young Corliss was born with two unusual birthmarks. One was a large mark to the right of his nose, just below the eye; the other was on his back. Both of these marks were located in the exact places where Vincent had been disfigured by surgical scars!

Corliss himself seemed to recall his previous life as Victor Vincent as well. When only thirteen months of age he called himself by Vincent's proper tribal name, and even queried his parents as to whether they remembered his 'promise'. Corliss also provided his bewildered parents with a long list of details about his previous life. Many of these details concerned incidents which even the Chotkins were unfamiliar with until they undertook to check out their son's statements.

On one occasion, for instance, Corliss told his parents that, as Vincent, he had run out of fuel while boating. To attract attention he had put on a Salvation Army uniform and was able to flag down a passing steamship. Only by looking into their relative's life in detail were the Chotkins able to verify this little episode.

In the meantime, Corliss also began to develop several personality traits and physical characteristics apparently inherited from Vincent. He developed his relative's fondness for tinkering with engines and displayed the elder man's peculiar shuffling walk.

However, the strongest type of evidence for reincarnation comes in those instances in which a child seems born with a *skill* apparently carried over from a previous life. One such skill is language. A language can only be acquired through exposure, practice, rehearsal, and cognitive awareness. Learning a language is akin to learning to ride a bike or to swim. It doesn't come easily, and one learns through trial and error. There just aren't any short-cuts. Yet there are a few cases on record of young children who, while recalling their past lives, also seem conversant in foreign languages to which they have never been exposed. Let us now look at one such case which was recently reported in Brazil, where it was uncovered by Hernani Andrade, one of South America's leading parapsychologists.[4]

Viviane Silvino was born in Sao Paulo in 1963. Though Portuguese by birth, the young girl soon astounded her parents and grandparents when she started bringing snatches of Italian into her conversation. Even before she was two years old, she was calling her sister *mia sorella*, and would call her doll *bambola*. Both of these expressions were correctly used and applied. And once when Viviane's mother was explaining to her washerwoman that she didn't know anyone who spoke Italian, the little girl exclaimed, 'Io parlo', which is correct for 'I speak it'. The girl even began correctly using rather obscure Italian words and expressions in her day-to-day conversation.

As Guy Lyon Playfair, an English-born journalist who studied the case from Andrade's own archives, writes in his book, *The Unknown Power*:

Once Silvia (Viviane) climbed into a pair of her mother's shoes and started clattering around the house. When Grandma told her to be quiet, she replied: 'Don't disturb me, I'm doing a *pestadura*'. This means nothing in Portuguese, but in Italian it is literally 'hard foot' or stomping, which was, indeed, what she was doing. Seeing her youngest sister lying in her pram, Sylvia commented on the fact that she was *losca*, or cross-eyed, the Portuguese for which is *vesgo*'

It was only somewhat after she had begun to work Italian words into her vocabulary that Viviane actually started to recall a past life. Up until this time, the only indication that the girl was being plagued by memories of a prior existence was manifest in her inexplicable fear of aeroplanes. But eventually the child recalled a life in Rome, and even offered the specific names of several of her friends of that time, recounted incidents from their lives, and dramatically recalled bombing raids over the city. This indicated that she had lived her previous life during World War II, thus explaining her fear of planes.

Unfortunately, attempts to trace Viviane's past life in Italy have so far proved unsuccessful. This shouldn't seem strange, though, since many public records were destroyed during the hideous war that wracked all Europe during the fitful forties. But her curious ability to command Italian cannot easily be dismissed by the sceptic.

Many people are convinced that these 'cases of the reincarnation-type', as Stevenson calls them, are unequivocal evidence supporting the rebirth doctrine, and if all cases of extracerebral memory were as neat and trim as the above three cases, perhaps this conclusion would be justifiable. But they aren't. Subsequent research undertaken by Dr Stevenson over the past few years indicates that the issue is much more complex than it might appear at first sight. Many cases of extracerebral memory are complicated by so many irregularities and paradoxes that 'simple' reincarnation just cannot explain them.

Cases that Cannot be Explained as 'Simple' Reincarnation
The case of Said Bouhamsy, also thoroughly investigated by Ian Stevenson, is a beautiful case in point. Bouhamsy was a Druse (a member of a Muslim sect that teaches reincarnation) who died in Lebanon in 1943 in a road accident. Six months later his sister gave birth to a son. When the boy first learned to speak, practically his first words were the proper names of Bouhamsy's children. The boy also described the truck accident which had ended his previous life and developed a phobia centring on trucks which lasted for many years. It was a splendid case of past-life recall except for one hitch. In 1958, in a town only twenty-five miles away, a lad named Imad Elawar was born. From the age of two he *also*

remembered a previous life apparently as Said Bouhamsy! He recalled the truck accident, remembered how many children he once had, and so on. And he, too, developed a morbid fear of trucks. He also spoke of a former mistress, Jumille, whom Stevenson ultimately discovered was the mistress not of Said Bouhamsy, but of his cousin.

So here we have a case in which *two* children recalled the *same* previous life. Obviously this type of case cannot be explained very easily as a 'simple' case of reincarnation.

And then there's the puzzling case of Jasbir Lal Jat, a three-and-a-half-year-old Indian boy who, after almost dying of smallpox in 1954, spontaneously began speaking about a previous life as Sobha Ram, who lived in a neighbouring village. He stated that his father's name was Shanka, that he had died from eating poisoned sweets during a wedding procession (which had caused him to fall from a cart), and many other true incidents in Ram's life. On being taken from his home in the Uttar Pradesh province of India to the neighbouring village of Vehedi, where Ram had lived, he correctly recognized several of his previous relatives and spoke to them in detail about his past life. All these details were checked and verified by Ian Stevenson during a field trip to India in 1961.

So here again we have what seems a beautiful case of reincarnation . . . except for one sobering fact. Sobha Ram didn't die before Jasbir was born. Ram's life only came to its abrupt end when the boy was fully three years old.

How can we explain this odd case? Is it an instance of genuine reincarnation? Spirit possession? Transmigration of the soul? Did Jasbir actually die during his bout with smallpox, during which time his body was reanimated by the soul of Sobha Ram? If nothing else, such cases alert us to the fact that instances of extracerebral memory are by no means cast-iron evidence for reincarnation. The data which can be gleaned from these cases just isn't clear-cut enough, and they are full of paradoxes that can't be overlooked.

There is another issue as well which few researchers of reincarnation-type cases have bothered to study. Yet it has a crucial bearing on any interpretation one might wish to apply to cases of extracerebral memory. Children talk about past lives more frequently in countries where the reincarnation doctrine is espoused. This phenomenon may be similar to the way children in our own culture often produce 'imaginary playmates'.* *In most cases these recollections are made-up stories which do*

---

*All too often students of the psychic field jump to the conclusion that 'imaginary playmates' are genuine apparitions, and as such, represent a form of psychic phenomena. Research suggests, however, that children produce these unseen companions in order to practise verbal skills, and that they are of a purely psychological nature.

not stand up to investigation. So the phenomenon of 'past-life recall' may be an inherently psychological one. Any theory concerning the nature of reincarnation-type cases must be capable of explaining why some manifestations of this phenomenon are evidential while others are not. Researchers such as Ian Stevenson have only focused their attention on the former type, and have thus given the public a rather one-sided picture of this multi-faceted enigma.

Professor C. T. K. Chari, a parapsychologist and teacher at Madras Christian College, India, has argued that *all* cases of past-life recall are basically psychological in nature, brought on by the child's exposure to the reincarnation doctrine. But it is quite feasible, he believes, that on *rare occasions* a child gifted with ESP might clairvoyantly and unconsciously latch on to genuine information about a recently deceased individual while his mind is developing a rebirth fantasy.[5]

This general theory is ingenious and can indeed explain why some cases of extracerebral memory are evidential, while others are not. It can also explain such 'oddities' as the Jasbir and Said Bouhamsy cases. Unfortunately, Professor Chari's theory cannot explain those cases in which children are born with birthmarks possessed by or inherited from their previous incarnations, nor can it explain how a child can speak a language to which he or she has never been exposed. Such a feat goes beyond the limits of ESP as we know it.

So the problem of whether or not cases of past-life recall can serve as evidence for reincarnation is currently deadlocked. Researchers who believe in reincarnation cannot explain the anomalies in their data; the sceptics cannot explain away the more evidential aspects of the rebirth mystery. What we need, then, is perhaps not more research on cases of the reincarnation type, but another method of exploring the reincarnation question, perhaps a way to deliberately and systematically explore someone's past life — assuming, of course, that he has experienced one. Does hypnosis present such a method?

Evidence from Hypnotic Regression

Using hypnosis to 'regress' a subject back to a previous life is not a new idea. In fact, it is almost impossible to tell just who first originated the procedure. We know that several French psychic investigators were toying with the technique at the turn of the century. But they didn't achieve very consistent results with it.

Perhaps the first modern case of a *spontaneous* 'past-life recall' achieved under hypnosis was recorded by William McDougall, the Harvard psychologist, back in the early part of the present century.[6] McDougall wasn't at all interested in reincarnation, but he was an expert on hypnosis and came across the incident in question while conducting some research on the hypnotic state at Oxford University in England. During an experiment with a particularly gifted hypnotic subject, the young man suddenly 'announced' that he was an Egyptian carpenter and described how he had been given the job of sculpting figures on tablets meant for a Pharaohnic tomb. He described the images he was creating in some detail. They included an eagle, a hand with a zig-zag insignia by it, a God with a white crown, and a figure representing the 'upper and lower' worlds. None of this made much sense to McDougall until nine months later when Sir Flinders Petrie, an English archaeologist working with the Egyptian Exploration Society, announced that he had just finished excavating the cenotaph of an obscure First Dynasty king of the Nile. All of the symbols described by McDougall's subject were found on the cenotaph. By checking dates, McDougall also discovered that the hypnotic session had been conducted at about the very time Petrie was making his initial discoveries.

The late Sir Cyril Burt, another eminent British psychologist, happened to be attending McDougall's experiment. He subsequently wrote that 'the student himself claimed to know nothing of ancient Egypt beyond what was in the Bible'. Because he was blind, the student's reading was extremely restricted as well, and he had therefore read nothing on ancient Egypt.

McDougall was never able to solve the mystery of his subject's Egyptian recollections. His only conclusion was that either the young man had unconsciously pieced the story together from bits and pieces of information he had learned over the years about Egyptian symbols (but had *consciously* forgotten), or that he had telepathically tapped Petrie's mind.

And that, in a nutshell, is the whole problem when trying to determine the authenticity of hypnotically recalled past-life memories. There seems little doubt that, under hypnosis, some people can come up with very accurate and convincing stories about the past lives they allegedly lived in distant eras and places. But are these genuine recollections of past lives? Or are they little fantasies which the unconscious mind can produce on demand by weaving together previously learned information, lost to conscious memory, but stored deep in the recesses of the mind? This phenomenon is technically called 'cryptomnesia', which means 'hidden memory'. Parapsychologists have also learned that hypnotized subjects often make especially good ESP subjects. So it is also possible that a hypnotically regressed subject might unconsciously use telepathy and clairvoyance to produce genuine information when constructing a past-life fantasy.

These issues were first raised in depth in 1956 when many parapsychologists began to debate openly whether hypnosis could genuinely be used as an aid in reincarnation research. This was the year that Morey Bernstein, a Colorado businessman and amateur hypnotist, caused a sensation with his book, *The Search for Bridey Murphy*. The book described how an ordinary Colorado housewife, Virginia Tighe (called Ruth Simmons in the book), had recalled a life as Bridey Murphy in nineteenth-century Ireland over the course of several regression sessions. During these sessions she had recalled the names of several relatives and historical sites, and even spoke with an Irish brogue. As soon as the case hit the press there were attempts to trace Bridey's life in Ireland. The results of these searches were published in *Life*, and in *American* magazine, and a whole series of reports on 'the search for Bridey Murphy' was syndicated in the Hearst newspaper chain. The result was that while *some* of the people and places Mrs Tighe mentioned during her trances were tracked down, other pieces of her story *seemed* to have been dramatizations of childhood experiences drawn from her own life or memories buried in her own mind. Even the name Bridey gave for her husband, Sean Brien MacCarthy, comes close to being an anagram for the name Morey Bernstein!

The Bridey Murphy mystery remains unsolved. But the case did serve to warn potential investigators about the enormous difficulties inherent in attempting to verify cases of hypnotically elicted past-life recalls. And this explains why very little research on the hypnotic exploration of reincarnation was published from 1956 until the very recent present. Even Dr Ian Stevenson, who is probably the leading authority on the reincarnation issue, has disparaged the use of hypnosis as a tool in reincarnation research.

This tide has begun to change, though, during the last few years. Once again at least a few researchers are turning to hypnosis as a method for investigating reincarnation. And some of these new investigations have uncovered some rather uncomfortable findings ... at least for the sceptics!

One such researcher was the late Arnold Bloxham, an English hypnotherapist who held a life-long interest in reincarnation. He began his research on reincarnation in about 1940, and carried out his investigations until the time of his death. Eventually the BBC became interested in his work and filmed a documentary on it. As a result, a BBC producer, Jeffrey Iverson, took pains to verify the memories of several of Bloxham's subjects.

Bloxham's star subject was a young woman named Jane Evans, who during the course of several sessions was able to recall no less than seven separate lives.[7] Among these was one in third-century York, another as a Jewess in twelfth-century York, one in fifteenth-century France, yet another as a handmaiden to Catherine of Aragon in the sixteenth century, a sixth life as a serving girl in London during the reign of Queen Anne, and a last existence as a nun in a Maryland (U.S.) convent. Mrs Evans had not originally come to Bloxham because of his research on reincarnation, but because of his ability to relieve rheumatism through hypnosis. She went to the hypnotherapist as a patient, not a subject. Bloxham, however, soon sensed that his new patient might make a good hypnotic subject, and thus began several months of regression work.

Jane's most outstanding past-life recall was that as a twelfth-century Jewess. During her regression she described the political situation of her day which ultimately led to the massacre of York's Jewish population in 1190, her family, and how they had to wear badges identifying them as Jews. Historically, all this material was either correct or consistent with what historians know of these dark days in English history. For example, in 1215 Church authorities in Rome announced that all Jews in Christian countries had to wear identifying insignias, although this practice had become widespread long before the turn of the thirteenth century. Jane also recalled several Jewish practices and anti-Jewish uprisings in England in astounding detail, including rather obscure information about Jewish money-lending traditions of the time. She even specifically mentioned the close money-lending connection between the Jewish communities in the districts of York and Lincoln. This, too, tallies with historical fact.

Nor should it be thought that the information Mrs Evans came up with under hypnosis was common knowledge. Most of it had to be verified by consulting Professor Barrie Dobson, an authority on Jewish history at York University.

The culmination of Jane's story was her hypnotic re-enactment, in agonizing detail, of the great Jewish massacre of 1190, when popular anti-semitism in York became so vicious that wholesale bloodshed broke out. Marauding bands broke into Jewish homes, murdering the occupants and stealing their possessions. Eventually, most of York's Jewish population was wiped out. She even described how the Jews ended up killing their own children rather than letting them fall victim to York residents. Jane ended her story by describing how she and her children sought refuge in a York church, where they hid in a crypt. There they were found and murdered.

Professor Dobson, who was allowed to hear the tapes of Jane's regressions, later told Jeffrey Iverson that her command of historical fact was 'impressively accurate' and that much of her information would most likely be known only to a few professional historians. He was also able to identify the church in which Jane had hidden with her family.

The massacre of Jews at York in 1190 was a vivid scene allegedly recalled by Arnold Bloxham's subject Jane Evans from a past life. (Mary Evans Picture Library)

Through various clues given in her account, he identified it as St Mary's Church in Castlegate. The church still stands today.

There was one flaw in Jane's story, though. St Mary's doesn't have a crypt or cellar — or, at least, so it was thought at the time of Bloxham's experiment. In fact, most English churches of the twelfth century were not built with crypts. However, a breakthrough in the Jane Evans case came six months after Professor Dobson had analysed Bloxham's regression tapes, when workmen renovating St Mary's accidentally discovered that the church *did* indeed have a crypt, *and that it had apparently been built before 1190!*

It is also interesting, as Professor Dobson has noted, that Jane Evans seems to remember rather obscure details about the massacre of 1190, yet has omitted all mention of the better-known (and thereby accessible to her through cursory historical research) facts about this black stain on English history.

Unfortunately, not all cases of hypnotically retrieved past-life recall bear scrutiny so well. Even the Jane Evans case is not pristine. Bloxham was able to revive her memories of another life in Roman times, but all the information she revealed was later traced to a novel she had read![8] And Melvin Harris, in *The Unexplained*, has persuasively argued that *all* her recollections can be traced to cryptomnesia — a conclusion accepted by both Dobson and Iverson. But there is another line of evidence for the reincarnation doctrine which has recently been obtained through hypnosis . . . and a possibly more important one.

Xenoglossy and the Case for Reincarnation

A very different way of exploring reincarnation through hypnosis is to see if a regressed subject can speak a foreign language which he has never learned in his current life during his past-life recall. This is a phenomenon which a few people who spontaneously recall previous incarnations have displayed on rare occasions. Technically called *xenoglossy*, it appears to be rare during hypnotic regression, but two cases have recently come to light that deserve careful examination.

The first is the widely publicized case of Delores Jay, a Virginia housewife whose story was reported in just about every paper in the country. It was thoroughly examined by Dr Ian Stevenson, who was impressed enough by it to write a report dealing with the case in the *Journal* of the American Society for Psychical Research in 1976. Revd Carroll Jay, a Methodist minister and Delores' husband, eventually wrote a full-length book on the case, *Gretchen, I Am*, which gives more details about the investigation.[9]

The strange case of Delores Jay began in 1970 when Revd Jay, an experienced hypnotherapist, was treating his wife's backaches. One night after she had fallen asleep, she suddenly mumbled, 'Gretchen, ich bin', which is German for 'Gretchen, I am'. Revd Jay was surprised since his wife had never learned and could not speak German. He therefore implemented hypnotic sessions with his wife, who would invariably become 'Gretchen Gottlieb' when entranced. Gretchen eventually told quite a story about her life in nineteenth-century Germany. She only spoke in German and explained that she had been murdered in a forest when she was only sixteen years old. Her communications were usually via short and rather ungrammatical sentences. Ian Stevenson learned about the case in 1971 and began his own investigation in September of that year. Stevenson, who is self-taught in German and speaks the language fluently, personally conversed with Gretchen on several occasions and procured correct responses to questions put to her.

He also collected the testimony of several German-speaking visitors who had also interrogated Gretchen in that language while taking part in the regression sessions. Mrs Jay also took a lie detector test during which she denied ever having studied German and passed with flying colours.

The case, notwithstanding these factors, is nonetheless extremely hard to analyse. Stevenson, on one hand, has remained greatly impressed by it. In his 1976 report, for instance, he points out that Mrs Jay introduced 237 German words during the course of several hypnotic sessions. (In other words, she spoke 237 words which had not been previously used in her presence by any German-speaking observers who had interviewed Gretchen while Mrs Jay was hypnotized.) Stevenson was also impressed by the Jays' openness in allowing an outside investigation into the case. However, the Virginia psychiatrist is not sure that the case is actually one of reincarnation. In his A.S.P.R. report he argues that 'spirit possession' might be an equally likely explanation for 'Gretchen Gottlieb', though he has not explained why hypnosis had to be used in order to contact her.

My own opinion of the case is not as positive as Stevenson's. In fact, after carefully perusing the published reports of the Gretchen Gottlieb case, my own verdict is rather negative. It seems likely, to me, that it is either one of cryptomnesia or fraud.

It may seem cruel to charge fraud, especially since the Jays have always co-operated with scientific investigators. However, this theory — even though Stevenson rejects it — cannot be easily dismissed. Even Revd Jay candidly admits in his book that on one occasion he learned that his wife had surreptitiously bought a German dictionary and wilfully faked one of the regressiion sessions. There are, however, many other aspects of the Gretchen Gottlieb case that make it suspect. Among these one might list:

1. All the historical facts Gretchen recalled were either false or could not be verified. Ian Stevenson himself points out this embarrassing fact in his report on the case.
2. Gretchen does not speak correct German. It is ungrammatical and sometimes poorly articulated.
3. Sometimes Gretchen would answer questions put to her in German with non sequiturs, indicating that she did not really understand what was being asked.
4. Gretchen often — and awkwardly — avoids using verbs in her sentences. When she does use them, she invariably speaks in the present tense and carefully shuns either past or future tenses even when her utterances call for them.

This fourth point strikes me as the most suspicious, since verb conjugations are the most difficult aspect of a language to master. A person faking a case of xenoglossy, either consciously or unconsciously, would probably have a difficult time correctly using tenses and would try to avoid them or use them in their most simple forms. This is exactly what Gretchen does quite consistently. And if we couple Gretchen's badly spoken German with her rather poor command of historical fact, the end result hardly makes a very good case for the reincarnation hypothesis.

A better case for reincarnation has recently been uncovered, though, by Dr Joel Whitton, a psychiatrist in Toronto, Canada. Whitton has been studying the subject of past-life regression since 1973 as a purely psychological phenomenon. He certainly never expected to come across a case of xenoglossy. But he did in 1976 when he began hypnotizing a 30-year-old psychologist, whose identity has yet to be publicly revealed.

Whitton's subject has so far remembered two lives as well as snatches of the languages he allegedly spoke during those incarnations.[10] The first life he has recalled was as a Viking who lived in about AD 1000. Unlike most regressed subjects, the psychologist does not literally 'become another personality' during his Viking incarnation. Instead, he sees images of his past life and hears his alter ego speaking to him and giving the answers to questions posed by his hypnotist. Over the course of several sessions, the psychologist has come out with several words in Norsk, an ancient language which is the precursor of Modern Icelandic. Interestingly enough, most of these words, when translated, have been found to refer to the sea and to sea life. These are, of course, just the type of words a reincarnated Viking might be expected to remember. A few words which seem to have Serbian or Russian roots have been uttered as well.

So far, though, the psychologist has not actually developed a full-scale secondary personality, such as Mrs Tighe's 'Bridey Murphy' or Mrs Jay's 'Gretchen Gottlieb'.

Whitton's subject has also recalled a life he lived as a young man in Mesopotamia in around AD 625. During this phase of his regression, he was able to write a few scripts of the language he spoke or wrote during this existence. These scripts have recently been identified by Indrahim Pourhadi, an expert in Near Eastern Languages at the Library of Congress in Washington, DC, as Sassanid Pahlavi. This is the very language which was spoken in Mesopotamia during the seventh century, and has no relationship to modern Iranian.

Dr Whitton has not as yet published a detailed report on the experiments with his unnamed subject. Nor has he published anything about the life stories these alter egos have told about themselves, nor any historical data they may have come up with. However, from the standpoint of evidence, Whitton's case represents a particularly strong case for reincarnation. The fact that his subject spoke and wrote two obscure and 'dead ' languages makes the case more impressive than most other instances of xenoglossy.

In conclusion, then, can hypnosis be used to explore the reincarnation question? And if so, how consistent is the technique?

The evidence — like that gleaned from cases of extracerebral memory — is contradictory. There is some evidence that hypnosis can help one recall a past life, but the evidence is subject to many different interpretations. It is especially difficult to judge what roles cryptomnesia and ESP play in the development of these recollections. Nor do most hypnotists experimenting with past-life recall procure very good results with it. Dr Whitton worked for several years, and with dozens of exceptionally good hypnotic subjects, before discovering his star performer.

There is some evidence, however, that the *state of mind* induced by hypnosis might be the key to reincarnation more than the technique itself. Hypnosis induces an altered state of consciousness. Some very tentative evidence exists that volunteer subjects, placed in altered states of consciousness, might have a peculiar propensity for remembering so-called past lives. One such state of mind can be induced through the use of what is called 'guided imagery'. This technique has been recently used with claimed success by Dr Helen Wambach, a Californian psychologist who uses it with whole groups of subjects.[11] She has recently reported on her research in her book, *Reliving Past Lives*. Dr Wambach first relaxes her subjects and then guides them, through suggestion, back through their present lives on a journey through which they explore their past lives as well. Only time will tell whether her subjects are really experiencing past-life recall or are only fantasizing. A more bizarre approach to reincarnation has accidentally been discovered by Dr Stanislav Grof, a Czech psychiatrist now working in the United States, as a by-product of his LSD research. In his book *Realms of the Human Unconscious,* he notes that a few of his subjects spontaneously recalled past lives as part of their LSD experiences. Sometimes they have come up with accurate information about those lives as well.[12]

Whatever the truth or fiction of the reincarnation doctrine, there is certainly no lack of researchers and techniques by which to explore it. Hopefully, they will in time produce results which give us less ambiguous evidence for or against survival after death.

8.

Some Personal Thoughts

No student of the psychic field can study the evidence for survival without coming to some personal conclusions. Parapsychologists rarely agree on very much and the survival issue is no exception. A few researchers adamantly reject the idea of survival, while a handful of others seem favourably disposed to the notion. The majority of parapsychologists, however, tend to remain simply (and safely) agnostic. Because of the very nature of the controversy, any conclusions a student of the field ultimately reaches must be partially subjective and totally individual.

The survival issue actually consists of two very separate aspects, since the existence of some sort of life after death does not necessarily imply that communication between the dead and the living is possible. So the controversy can be broken down in the survival aspect *proper* and its spiritistic corollary. I personally believe that the latter is the more fruitful area of exploration, since any data bearing on it also bears critically on the former.

My own sentiments are decidedly favourable to the survival notion, although I am no longer as firm about my position as I was ten years or so ago. There is more and more evidence accumulating to suggest that out-of-body experiences are only rarely veridical; that near-death survivors might be responding to auditory cues (provided by doctors and nurses) when they experience their souls leaving the body; and that deathbed visions could well be archetypal psychological experiences. These lines of sceptical inquiry and thinking have certainly not robbed these phenomena of their importance, but they suggest that we should keep our scepticism well-honed. A good lesson might be learned from the mass of research poured into the study of the out-of-body experience during the years following the Kidd bequest. If nothing else, the combined weight of this research showed that the OBE is not as clear-cut and discrete a phenomenon as we had thought. Some of the evidence directly suggested that some aspect of the mind can temporarily leave the body;

but the results of other projects failed to isolate anything consistent or measurable about this 'aspect'. Rarely is anything clear-cut in parapsychology, which is one reason why the survival issue has long remained so controversial.

What kind of data can serve as evidence for survival, then? Many researchers believe that no single line of evidence nor single case study *can* prove the validity of the survival hypothesis. The evidence, they argue, must be evaluated as a whole and as an intertwining complex of facts, figures and cases.

The crucial issue researchers face today is actually the same one parapsychologists grappled with in the 1880s and well into the 1920s. Do any cases exist that cannot be explained as the result of our own ESP capabilities? The super-ESP hypothesis states that our ESP powers are not constrained by any limiting factors. It may have access to any piece of infomation or complex of information existing anywhere in the world, its past or present. This information can then be processed unconsciously before being presented into consciousness by way of a 'spiritistic' message. Spirit communicators, trance personalities and deathbed visions may therefore be projections from our own minds, carefully structured through the collection of psychic information.

The idea that we possess super-ESP is only a theory, and it is one that has come in for a fair share of criticism of late. But there is also considerable evidence that ESP can succeed at very complex tasks in the laboratory. So while the idea of super-ESP may seem extravagant, it follows logically from what parapsychologists have learned about the sixth sense. For this reason I prefer to adopt the idea that the ultimate evidence for survival rests on only two types of cases:

1.   Spontaneous cases of post-mortem contact in which the motivation for the communication rests more with the deceased agent than with the witness.
2.   Cases in which the witness suddenly develops or takes on a skill possessed by the deceased agency. There is simply no evidence that ESP can be used to acquire a skill. ESP is an information channel, while a skill is a learned attribute developed through practice.

Two classic cases fitting these criteria exist within parapsychology's rich literature, and a good case for survival could be based on either of them.

Probably the most celebrated case of spontaneous contact with the dead was the Chaffin Will affair, which was first reported in 1927.[1] The report concerned the North Carolina estate of James L. Chaffin who died in 1921. The terms of his will stated that his property should go to his third son (Marshall), which left his wife and three other sons virtually disinherited. This document was written and witnessed in 1905. The terms of the will were carried out, but in 1925 — four years after his death — Chaffin's apparition began appearing to one of his other sons, James P. Chaffin, Jr. The apparition materialized by the young man's bedside dressed in an old overcoat he had often worn in life. The figure only spoke on the occasion of its second appearance. Its message was that, 'You will find my will in my overcoat pocket.' This overcoat was in the possession of yet another brother. The lining of the coat was sewn up and a handwritten note was found inside which simply said: 'Read the 27th chapter of Genesis in my daddie's old Bible.' The search was on again. The bible was located in the possession of Chaffin's widow and it was examined in front of two independent witnesses. No one was very surprised when a rough handwritten will dated 1919 was found there. This testament divided the estate equally among the Chaffin children. The will was presented in court, upheld, and the Chaffin estate redistributed. The authenticity of the will was so unchallengeable that Marshall's family didn't contest it.

The standard non-survivalistic explanation for this case is that James P. Chaffin simply learned about the will through clairvoyance. His unconscious mind then produced the apparition as a mediating vehicle through which the information could be relayed into consciousness. This theory may seem glib, but it really cannot explain many of the main features of the case. For instance, it can't explain why the information only emerged four years after Chaffin's death and not immediately after the terms of the will were first made known, when James P. Chaffin's motivation to learn about the will would have been at its peak. Nor can any sort of super-ESP theory explain why young Chaffin's ESP powers focused on the overcoat pocket and not directly on the bible. And why did the communication confuse the message in the overcoat pocket with the will itself? Remember, the apparition said that the *will* was in the overcoat pocket. This was not literally true. Some commentators on the case also overlook the fact that even after the will was found, the apparition of James Chaffin appeared a final time. He was still apparently concerned about the injustice to his family.

Now if we assume that James Chaffin really *was* speaking from beyond the veil, all the oddities in the case begin to make perfect sense. We know that memory is often a fragile power and that two obviously related memories can easily become confused over time. The deceased Chaffin could easily have become confused between the will and the message he had left in his overcoat pocket. In fact, I feel that this little bit of confusion can *only* be explained by accepting that James Chaffin's surviving personality was the source of the information. The survival theory can also explain why the apparition appeared after the will was found . . . at a time when James P. Chaffin no longer had any need or motivation to produce the apparition. The deceased man may simply have been unaware that the will was now in his family's possession.

Many of these same motivational factors can be found in the Teresita Basa case, where the surviving personality of the murdered woman had a greater motivation to see justice done than Mrs Chua probably did. Mrs Chua hadn't known Teresita very well and she wasn't even working at the hospital when the critical messages were received. She therefore wasn't in any immediate danger from the murderer, who was still working on the staff.

Now to turn our attention to the second type of case I cited above. Cases of people who have suddenly developed unusual skills after allegedly making contact with the dead are rare. Only a few such cases appear in the literature, but some of them are extremely impressive. There are several reports in the older literature on mediumship concerning trance mediums who suddenly began speaking in foreign languages. These were languages familiar to the 'communicators' speaking through them, but beyond the knowledge or skill of the sensitives. This phenomenon was more commonly reported from the spiritualist press than from the 'official' reports of the S.P.R., so 'polyglot' mediumship was not documented as thoroughly as it could have been. Nonetheless, a few cases still managed to hold up under critical scrutiny.[2]

Today in our own times, psychics gifted with unusual skills inherited from their 'spirit' contacts abound:

1. Rosemary Brown is an English lady who composes sometimes excellent music under the tutelage of Europe's great composers of the past. She has little formal musical training, yet even many musicologists have been impressed by the quality of her productions.
2. Emma Conti is an Italian psychic who 'receives' poetry from the spirit of Emily Dickinson. She has won forty-six literary awards for her poetry, even though she never even attended high school.
3. Matthew Manning is best known today as a psychic healer. When his powers first developed in England when he was a teenager, he began drawing detailed and exquisite etchings in the style of several deceased artists.

The problem with all of these cases is the same, though. Psychology knows relatively little about our creative capacities, or the nature of unconscious creativity, so it is virtually impossible to trace the true source of these inspired powers. Just because some psychics believe that their creations come from the spirit world doesn't necessarily make it so. It should be noted, though, that both Rosemary Brown and Emma Conti have purportedly channelled through evidential messages from their 'spirit' contacts.

There does exist, nonetheless, a very similar case in the historical annals of psychic science that overcomes this problem.

The now famous Thompson/Gifford case dates back to 1905.[3] Frederic Thompson was born in Massachusetts in 1868 and worked as a jeweller. He was also a Sunday painter of sorts, though only a mediocre one. Sometime in 1905 he suddenly found his mind and body invaded by a foreign intelligence. He developed an overwhelming urge to sketch and paint and soon began attributing these compulsions to his alter ego, whom he named 'Mr Gifford'. He adopted the name from Robert Swain Gifford, a celebrated landscape artist whom he had met on two occasions out in the country near New Bedford. These compulsions were often accompanied by visionary landscapes which served as the models for his paintings. Some of the resulting artistic achievements surmounted anything created by virtue of his own meagre talents, but it wasn't until he learned about Gifford's death that he became concerned about his sanity. When Thompson discovered that his strange compulsions developed shortly after Gifford's death, he sought out Professor James H. Hyslop at the American Society for Psychical Research in New York. Hyslop was not too impressed by Thompson's story and at first believed the case would contribute more to the burgeoning field of abnormal psychology than to psychical research. Despite this, his interest was sufficiently aroused for him to explore Thompson's claims further. Hyslop was primarily interested in the art work, so in 1907 he took possesion of several of Thompson's paintings and sketches for further analysis.

These paintings became the focal point of the case, for several art experts who saw them spontaneously remarked on their similarity to the work of the late R. Swain Gifford. But the true dénouement of the case came when Hyslop and Thompson began exploring the life and work of the deceased artist. They eventually discovered that some of the sketches now in Hyslop's possession matched unfinished paintings left by the artist at the time of his death. They were still in the possession of his widow, who had never shown them publicly. She had kept them at their long-time residence on a privately owned island just off the New England coast. Some of Thompson's other sketches were of actual locations later found on the island.

The strange case of Frederic Thompson is more complex than any brief summary can communicate. Professor Hyslop was also

Frederic Thompson's sketch closely matches the unfinished painting by Robert Swain Gifford, 1907. (Mary Evans Picture Library)

experimenting with several trance mediums in Boston, New York and Virginia during these months. He began receiving several evidential messages from R. Swain Gifford, while Frederic Thompson found himself suddenly undergoing odd out-of-body experiences. It looked as if the deceased artist was trying to prove his identity through any channel available to him.

My own opinion about this extraordinary case is fairly clear-cut. Even if we entertain the possibility that Frederic Thompson was a powerful psychic, there seems no motivation for why he suddenly assimilated Gifford's personality in so bizarre a manner. The deceased artist would have had a greater motivation to continue on with his work, and naturally he would have chosen a fellow artist (of sorts) whose hand he could most readily guide. It is also hard to fathom why Thompson began undergoing out-of-body experiences during this time, though this development is perfectly explicable if we assume that Gifford was attempting to control and possess him. The connection with Gifford's sudden intrusion in his life also explains Thompson's sudden artistic genesis.

Impressive reports of similar cases of 'spirit' return highlighted the early literature of psychical research. It is certainly a pity that cases of similar quality are uncommon today. This may result from the fact that contemporary parapsycholgists simply aren't as interested in ferreting them out and investigating them as were the founders of the field. I can well imagine how a researcher today would respond to the claims of someone like Frederic Thompson. The whole case looked very much like one of bizarre psychopathology. The psychic underpinnings of the events were only revealed because Hyslop decided to explore the case in further depth despite his initial cynicism. Researchers today rarely have the time or inclination to look into such cases so thoroughly. It is certainly interesting and revealing that not a single parapsychologist investigated the Teresita Basa case even after it had achieved nationwide publicity!

Just about the only contemporary researcher interested in studying cases bearing on the survival issue is Dr Ian Stevenson at the University of Virginia. Since he has been focusing on reincarnation-type cases, his contributions to other areas of survival research have been minimal. Recently, though, he and his colleague, Dr Satwant Pasricha, have issued a report on a third case for which only the survival theory seems a tenable explanation. This report concerns the strange trances of Uttara Huddar, a teacher and administrator in Nagpur, India.[4] She has been undergoing episodes since 1973 in which she takes on the personality and 'becomes' a woman named Sharada who lived in nineteenth-century Bengal. These trances can last from a few hours to several days and 'Sharada' has communicated a number of details about her life and her relations. Detailed genealogical research has proved that many of the names she has offered designate people who really existed in the Bengal district years ago. It is extremely doubtful that Ms Huddar could have had access to this information. 'Sharada' also speaks in Bengali, which is a dialect distinct from the Marathi tongue spoken by Ms Huddar. Experts have testified that Sharada speaks the language correctly and uses a vocabulary consistent with someone from the nineteenth century. Ms Huddar

Descriptions of death and survival are consistent across cultural frontiers: this anonymous Chinese print shows the astral body separated from the physical body but still connected by a cord. (Mary Evans Picture Library)

apparently once had some passing familiarity with written Bengali script, but not with the spoken language.

The case of Sharada's uncanny return is still unfolding, and it is destined to become a classic. The only problem is whether or not it is an example of reincarnation or genuine spirit possession. Dr Stevenson prefers the former theory, although any decision on the matter would be arbitrary. The important point is that some form of survival is implied by adopting either explanation.

Despite such cases, I don't think that the survival controversy will ever really be definitively resolved by any single case or line of future research. I believe the real case for survival lies buried in the field's rich archives and historical literature. It is interesting to note that two of the three cases outlined in this chapter date back well over fifty years to the true heyday of survival research. The cases and studies made during those years outstrip much of the related work coming out of parapsychology today. Although my views have vacillated considerably over the years, I still find the survival theory to be the most cogent explanation for some of these cases. But merely coming to the personal opinion that we ultimately survive death is really not an end in itself. It only leads one to ask a host of even more provocative and difficult questions:

What aspect of the personality actually survives?

Do we possess a soul, or is just a complex of personality traits and drives released at death?

Do we survive death permanently, or do we undergo a second and more permanent annihilation?

What is the nature of the 'next' world?

These are the true essentials of the survival issue, but they are issues upon which parapsychology has little right to comment. Precious little evidence from the field's past or present literature sheds any light on them.

To me, the greatest mystique of the survival controversy is just this fundamental impenetrability. Because of its very nature, I doubt if the issue will ever be resolved to everyone's satisfaction. That time will only come when we discover a reliable method by which we can consistently contact the dead, and that day will probably never come. It is obvious that the human mind is too complex and inconsistent a tool to use, but nothing better seems to be on the immediate horizon. So parapsychology's best bet would be to explore further those lines of evidence already under consideration. There is still much we need to learn about trance mediumship, near-death and related out-of-body experiences, deathbed visions and cases of the reincarnation type. Perhaps some day a case of post-mortem contact will come to light so staggering and impressive that whether we survive the shock of death will no longer be in question. But I can't honestly say whether this is a genuine possibility or merely a momentary exercise in unabashed speculation or optimism.

The case for survival is impressive, but not yet proven.

References

Chapter 1   Psychical Research and the Survival Controversy
1. Fuller, John. *The Great Soul Trial.* New York: Macmillan, 1969.
2. Gurney, Edmund, Myers, F. W. H. and Podmore, Frank, *Phantasms of the Living.* London: Trubner, 1886.
3. Gauld, Alan. *The Founders of Psychical Research.* New York: Schocken, 1968.
4. Piper, Alta. *The Life and Work of Mrs Piper.* London: Kegan Paul, 1929.
5. Hodgson, Richard. A record of certain phenomena of trance. *Proceedings*: Society for Psychical Research, 1892, 8, 1-167.
6. Myers, F. W. H.; Lodge, Oliver; Leaf, W.; James, William. A record of observations of certain phenomena of trance. *Proceedings*: Society for Psychical Research, 1890, 6, 436-659.
7. Hodgson, Richard. A further record of observations of certain phenomena of trance. *Proceedings*: Society for Psychical Research, 1898, 284-582.
8. Ibid.
9 Saltmarsh, H. F. *Evidence of Personal Survival from Cross-Correspondences.* London: Bell, 1938.
10. Thouless, Robert. *From Anecdote to Experiment in Psychical Research.* London: Routledge and Kegan Paul, 1972.
11. Lodge, Oliver. *Raymond.* New York: Doran, 1916.
12. Radclyffe-Hall, Ann and Una, Lady Troubridge. On a series of sittings with Mrs Osborne Leonard. *Proceedings*: Society for Psychical Research, 1920, 30, 339-554.
13. Thomas, C. Drayton. *Some New Evidence for Human Survival.* New York: Dutton, n.d.

Chapter 2   Mind Out of Body
1. Twemlow, S; Gabbard, G; and Jones, F. The out-of-body experience: I. phenomenology. Paper presented at the 1980 meeting of the American Psychiatric Association.

2. Tart, Charles C. A psychophysiological study of out-of-body experiences in a selected subject. *Journal* of the American Society for Psychical Research, 1968, 62, 3-27.

3. Mitchell, Janet. Out-of-the-body Vision. *Psychic* magazine, April, 1973.

4. Swann, Ingo. *To Kiss Earth Good-Bye*. New York: Hawthorn, 1975.

5. Osis, Karlis. Out-of-body research at the American Society for Psychical Research. *Newsletter* of the American Society for Psychical Research, 1974, No. 22.

6. Tanous, Alex. *Beyond Coincidence*. Garden City, N.Y.: Doubleday, 1976.

7. Rogo, D. Scott. Experiments with Blue Harary. In *Mind Beyond the Body* edited by D. Scott Rogo. New York: Penguin, 1978.

8. Targ, Russell and Puthoff, Harold. *Mind-Reach*. New York: Delacorte, 1973.

Chapter 3   Documenting the Near-Death Experience

1. Bradshaw, Rick. Personal reflections on near-death experiences. *Anabiosis*, 1979, 1 (2),11.

2. Tiegel, Eliot. His 'deaths' transformed the course of his life. *Los Angeles Times,* 30 May 1983.

3. Kastenbaum, Robert. Temptations from the everafter. *Human Behavior,* 1977, 6, 28-33.

4. Sabom, Michael and Kreutziger, Sarah. Physicians evaluate the near-death experience. *Theta*, 1978, 6, No. 4, 1-6.

5. Sabom, Michael. *Recollections of Death*. New York/San Francisco: Harper & Row, 1982.

6. Ring, Kenneth. *Life at Death*. New York: Coward, McCann and Georghegan, 1983.

7. Ring, Kenneth. Denver cardiologist discusses findings after 17 years of near-death research. *Anabiosis*, 1979, 1 (1), 1-2.

8. Rawlings, Maurice. *Beyond Death's Door.* New York: Bantam, 1978.

9. Garfield, Charles. More grist for the mill: additional near-death research findings and discussion. *Anabiosis*, 1979, 1 (1), 5-7.

Chapter 4   Spontaneous Contact with the Dead

1. Sussman, Lesley. Did voice from grave name killer? *Fate*, 1978, 31 (7), 61-7.

2. Mercado, Carol and O. A. *A Voice from the Grave*. Oak Park, Ill: Carolando Press, 1979.

3. Thacher, George A. and Hyslop, James. The case of Lieut. James B. Sutton. *Journal* of the American Society for Psychical Research, 1911, 5, 597-664.

4. Voice of murdered son led him to suspect, father says. *U.P.I.* 30 May 1970.

5. Kalish, Richard A. and Reynolds, David K. Widows view death: a brief research note. *Omega — the journal of death and dying,* 1974, 5, 187-92.
6. Kalish, Richard A. Contacting the dead: does group identification matter? In *Between Life and Death* edited by Robert Kastenbaum, New York: Springer, 1979.
7. Greely, Andrew. *Death and Beyond.* Chicago: Thomas More Press, 1976.
8. Burton, Julian. Contact with the dead: a common experience? *Fate,* 1982, 35 (4), 65-72.
9. Burton, Julian. *Survivors' Subjective Experience of the Deceased.* Doctoral dissertation: International College, 1980.
10. Solem, Helen. Do we contact the dead in our dreams? *Fate,* 1984, 37 (3), 79-84.
11. Osis, Karlis and Haraldsson, Erlendur. *At the Hour of Death.* New York: Avon, 1977.
12. Osis, Karlis. Characteristics of purposeful action in an apparition case. Paper delivered at the 26th annual convention of the Parapsychological Association, August 9-13, 1983.

Chapter 5   Tape-Recorded 'Spirit' Voices: Delusion or Breakthrough?
1. Roll, W. G. Spirit voices of Freidrich Jurgensen. *Report* No. 8 of the Psychical Research Foundation, Durham, N. Carolina, n.d.
2. Bayless, Raymond. Letter to the editor. *Journal* of the American Society for Psychical Research, 1959, 53, 35-9.
3. Raudive, Konstantine. *Breakthrough.* New York: Taplinger, 1971.
4. Ellis, David. Tape recordings of the dead? *Psychic,* 1974, 5, 44-9.
5. Smith, Susy. *Voices of the Dead?* New York: New American Library, 1977.
6. Meek, George. Spiricom: electronic communications with the 'dearly departed'. *New Realities,* 1983, 4, 8-15.
7. Rogo, D. Scott. *In Search of the Unknown.* New York: Taplinger, 1977.

Chapter 6   Phone-Calls from the Dead?
1. Burgess, Anthony. *Beard's Roman Women.* London: Hutchinson, 1976.
2. Smith, Susy. *The Power of the Mind.* Radnor, Pa.: Chilton, 1976.

Chapter 7   Reincarnation Reconsidered
1. Lenz, Frederick, *Lifetimes.* New York: Bobbs-Merrill, 1979.
2. Stevenson, Ian. Some new cases suggestive of reincarnation. V. the case of Indika Guneratne. *Journal* of the American Society for Psychical Research, 1974, 68, 58-90.

3. Stevenson, Ian. *Twenty Cases Suggestive of Reincarnation*. New York: American Society for Psychical Research, 1966.

4. Playfair, Guy Lyon. *The Unknown Power*. New York: Pocket Books, 1975.

5. Chari, C. T. K. Reincarnation research: method and interpretation. In *The Signet Handbook of Parapsychology* edited by Martin Ebon. New York: New American Library, 1978.

6. Van Over, Raymond and Oteri, Laura, eds. *William McDougall — Explorer of the Mind*. New York: Garrett Publications, 1969.

7. Iverson, Jeffrey. *More Lives than One?* New York: Warner, 1976.

8. Wilson, Ian. *All in the Mind*. Garden City, New York: Doubleday, 1982.

9. Jay, Carroll E. *Gretchen, I Am*. New York: Wyden Books, 1977.

10. Whitton, Joel. Xenoglossia: a subject with two possible instances. *New Horizons*, 1978, 2 (4), 18-26.

11. Wambach, Helen. *Reliving Past Lives*. New York/San Francisco: Harper & Row, 1978.

12. Grof, Stanislav. *Realms of the Human Unconscious*. New York: Viking, 1975.

Chapter 8   Some Personal Thoughts

1. Reported in the *Proceedings* of the Society for Psychical Research, 1927, 36, 517-24.

2. Bozzano, Ernesto. *Polyglot Mediumship*. London: Rider, n.d.

3. Hyslop, James H. A case of veridical hallucinations. *Proceedings* of the American Society for Psychical Research, 1909, 3, 1-469.

4. Stevenson, Ian, and Pasricha, S. A preliminary report on an unusual case of the reincarnation type with xenoglossy. *Journal* of the American Society for Psychical Research, 1980, 74, 331-48.

Bibliography and Reading List

Out-of-Body Experiences
Black, David, *Ekstacy: Out-of-body experiences*. Indianapolis: Bobbs-Merrill, 1975.
Blackmore, Susan. *Beyond the Body*. London: Heinemann, 1982.
Crookall, Robert. *The Study and Practice of Astral Projection*. Wellingborough: Aquarian Press, 1961.
—— *More Astral Projections*. Wellingborough: Aquarian Press, 1964.
Green, Celia. *Out-of-Body Experiences*. London: Hamish Hamilton, 1968.
Greenhouse, Herbert. *The Astral Journey*. Garden City, N.Y.: Doubleday, 1975.
Rogo, D. Scott (ed.) *Mind Beyond the Body*. New York: Penguin, 1978.
Smith, Susy. *The Enigma of Out-of-Body Travel*. New York: Helix Press, 1965.

Near-Death Experiences
Gabbard, Glen and Twemlow, S. W. *With the Eyes of the Mind*. New York: Praeger, 1985.
Gallup, George. *Adventures in Immortality*. New York: McGraw-Hill, 1982.
Lundahl, Craig. *A Collection of New-Death Research Readings*. Chicago: Nelson-Hall, 1982.
Osis, Karlis and Haraldsson, Erlendur. *At The Hour of Death*. New York: Avon, 1977.
Ring, Kenneth. *Life at Death*. New York: Coward, McCann, Georghegan, 1980.
Sabom, Michael. *Recollections of Death*. New York: Harper & Row, 1982.

Apparitions
Bayless, Raymond. *Apparitions and Survival of Death*. Secaucus, N.Y.: University Books, 1973.
Green, Celia and McCreery, Charles. *Apparitions*. London: Hamish Hamilton, 1975.

Jaffe, Aniela. *Apparitions and Precognition.* New Hyde Park, N.Y.: University Books, 1983.

McKenzie, Andrew. *Hauntings and Apparitions.* London: William Heinemann, 1982.

Rogo, D. Scott. *Phantoms.* Newton Abbott: David & Charles, 1976.

Tyrrell, G. N. M. *Apparitions.* New York: Collier, 1963.

Electronic Communication with the Dead

Bander, Peter. *Carry on Talking.* Gerrards Cross: Colin Smythe, 1972.

Raudive, Konstantine. *Breakthrough.* Gerrards Cross: Colin Smythe, 1971.

Rogo, D. Scott and Bayless, Raymond. *Phone Calls from the Dead.* London: New English Library, 1980.

Smith, Susy. *Voices of the Dead?* New York: New American Library, 1977.

Mediumship

Gauld, Alan. *Mediumship and Survival.* London: William Heinemann, 1982.

Gibbs, E. B. *They Survive.* London: Rider & Co., 1946.

Leonard, Gladys Osborne. *My Life in Two Worlds.* London: Cassell & Co., 1931.

Piper, Alta I. *The Life and Work of Mrs Piper.* London: Kegan Paul, Trench, Trubner and Co., 1929.

Salter, W. H. *Zoar.* London: Sidgwick & Jackson, 1961.

Saltmarsh, H.F. *Evidence of Personal Survival from Cross-Correspondences.* London: Bell, 1938.

Smith, Susy. *The Mediumship of Mrs Leonard.* New Hyde Park, N.Y.: University Books, 1964.

Thomas, Charles Drayton. *Some New Evidence for Human Survival.* New York: Dutton, n.d.

Survival, General

Beard, Paul. *Survival of Death.* London: Hodder & Stoughton, 1966.

Cummins, Geraldine. *Mind in Life and Death.* Wellingborough: Aquarian Press, 1956.

Ducasse, C. J. *A Critical Examination of the Belief in Life after Death.* Springfield, Ill.: Charles C. Thomas, 1961.

Hart, Hornell. *The Enigma of Survival.* Springfield, Ill.: Charles C. Thomas, 1956.

Jacobson, Nils O. *Life without Death.* New York: Delacorte, 1973.

McAdams, Elizabeth and Bayless, Raymond. *The Case for Life after Death.* Chicago: Nelson-Hall, 1981.

Rogo, D. Scott. *The Welcoming Silence.* Secaucus, N.J.: University Books, 1973.

Reincarnation

Ebon, Martin (ed.) *Reincarnation in the Twentieth Century.* New York: World, 1969.

Iverson, Jeffrey. *More Lives than One?* London: Souvenir Press, 1976.

Lenz, Frederick. *Lifetimes.* New York: Bobbs-Merrill, 1979.

Moss, Peter and Keeton, Joe. *Encounters with the Past.* Garden City, N.Y.: Doubleday, 1981.

Rogo, D. Scott. *The Search for Yesterday.* Englewood Cliffs, N. J.: Prentice-Hall, 1985.

Stevenson, Ian. *Twenty Cases Suggestive of Reincarnation.* New York: American Society for Psychical Research, 1966.

Wambach, Helen. *Reliving Past Lives.* New York: Harper & Row, 1978.

Wilson, Ian. *All in the Mind.* Garden City, N.Y.: Doubleday, 1981.

Index

ASSAP (Association for the Scientific Study of Anomalous Phenomena) was founded in 1981 to bring together people working in different fields of anomaly research. It does not compete with other societies or organizations, but serves as a link organization enabling members of existing groups to share views and information and benefit from pooled resources. ASSAP issues its own publications, has its own research archives, library and other facilities, and holds periodic public conferences and training events in various parts of the country: ASSAP co-operates with local groups or, where none exists, may form one of its own.

ASSAP members include people from all walks of life who share a belief that it is the scientific approach which is most likely to solve these enigmas: they are neither uncritical 'believers' on the one hand, nor blinkered sceptics on the other, but are ready to go where the evidence leads them. If you sympathize with this attitude and would like to participate actively in our exciting pursuit of the truth, you may consider joining us. Write for fuller details to the Editor c/o Aquarian Press, Denington Estate, Wellingborough NN8 2RQ.